Architecture Iconographies  *Survey*

# Architecture Iconographies   *Survey*   Matthew Wells

🔲 PARK BOOKS     Drawing Matter

Measuring Possibility   9

Surveys in Practice   33

*John Soane: The Construction Site*   35

*C R Cockerell: The Survey of Antiquity*   45

*Hippolyte Lebas, Henri Labrouste: The Envoi de Rome*   55

*Viollet-le-Duc: Landscapes and Restoration*   61

*Detmar Blow: The Modern Architect*   67

*Peter Märkli: The Search for Certainty*   75

Plates   89

An architect goes to a building, and wanting to record what they see, they take a bundle of folded sheets from their bag, searching in vain for a blank piece of paper. On these sheets are other drawings: the ground plan of an extension to an existing house annotated by many hands; a series of geometric diagrams of Baroque churches; a photocopy of an ordnance survey map showing the possible locations of a new structure. The pages are stuffed into a notebook filled with sketches from a trip abroad, a measured drawing of a window that needs replacing, and details from a site visit with students. In one way or another, all of these drawings are surveys. Each enables an architect to examine certain conditions of the built environment, whether geometric, relational, material or technical.

*Survey* emerged from a desire to examine this practice and its many forms to show how these very conventions might inform the practice of architecture today. I began not with one particular survey but with the entire collection of Drawing Matter, located in southwest England. Here, drawings are stored in the same room in which they are viewed, in contrast to institutional collections where works on paper are requested and generally examined one at a time. In this respect, Drawing Matter offers a unique opportunity to view the history of the discipline, not sheet by sheet, but all at once – from its beginnings in sixteenth-century Italy through to contemporary examples. These conditions reward an intuitive and associative approach. And so while I may have started by identifying the collection's archetypal survey drawings, such as C R Cockerell's study of the Parthenon or a careful survey by Alberto Ponis, other, more surprising examples, by Álvaro Siza and Peter Märkli, soon joined them. Such combinations allowed me to outline (and perhaps even establish) the rules for making a survey – and then to stretch them.

This book is, emphatically, not comprehensive. But, like all the best surveys, it sets out to convey a specific point of view – to show that while there are myriad processes for making a survey, the outcomes are as idiosyncratic as their authors. And so, if what follows is, at first glance a kind of survey in and of itself, informed by a particular collection, it is also a provocation to expand our understanding of the survey as not only a record of what is there, but as a way of imagining what might be.

*Matthew Wells*

*Measuring Possibility*

Unknown author, 'The Bellman's Chart', from *The Hunting of the Snark: An Agony in Eight Fits*, by Lewis Carroll, 1891 edition. Ink on paper, 190×130 mm

Lewis Carroll's 1876 nonsense poem, *The Hunting of the Snark (An Agony of Eight Fits)*, tells the story of the Bellman and his crew as they search the high seas for their elusive quarry. To navigate the waters, the shipmates rely on the Bellman's Chart. No ordinary nautical map marked with depths and currents, submerged hazards and places for safe harbour, this seems to be nothing more than an empty black frame drawn on the page; the blank space it delineates is the ocean. The crew are surprisingly elated to be guided by such an object, a navigational chart 'they could all understand':

'Other maps are such shapes, with their islands and capes!
But we've got our brave Captain to thank'
(So the crew would protest) 'that he's bought *us* the best –
A perfect and absolute blank!'

Take another look at the Bellman's Chart. Is it in fact blank? Or awash with information? Printed around the frame of the ocean is an array of cartographic terms – an incomplete set of cardinal directions, coordinates, horizon lines, poles, a scale bar that refers to nothing. These annotations, which seem to have been arbitrarily placed either by the book's illustrator, Henry Holiday, or by Carroll himself via a typesetter, still tell us many things: what we are looking at (an 'Ocean-Chart'), how to read it, and the fact that the territory in question is not empty at all, but full of possibility.

There is a risk in beginning an essay about the architectural survey with a nonsensical ocean chart of a non-existent place. Does something so spartan, with its pair of black frames barely signalling it as a drawing, even register on the spectrum of surveys included here? Graphically, the Bellman's Chart could scarcely be more distinct from the mapping in Eugène-Emmanuel Viollet-le-Duc's *Le massif du Mont Blanc*, published the same year as Carroll's poem. Comparing the two, we have one drawing that seems to show us nothing, and another that tries to reveal everything through highly detailed topographical views and analytical studies. Yet both find common ground – in their clear definitions of the site, in the annotations and symbols on the page and, not least, in their absurdity, one charting the seas by void, the other attempting quixotically to make visible every peak and col within the great massif.

What both the Bellman's Chart and Viollet-le-Duc's geographical study suggest is that while there are many ways to make a survey, the point of this type of drawing is to help us better understand not only what is evident, but also *how* we see it. Whether outlined on a sheet

NORTH

LATITUDE

EQUATOR

Scale of Miles.

TORRID ZONE

SOUTH POLE

MERIDIAN

EQUINOX

WEST

EAST

NORTH POLE

ZENITH

NADIR

LONGITUDE

LATITUDE

EQUATOR

Scale of Miles.

## OCEAN-CHART.

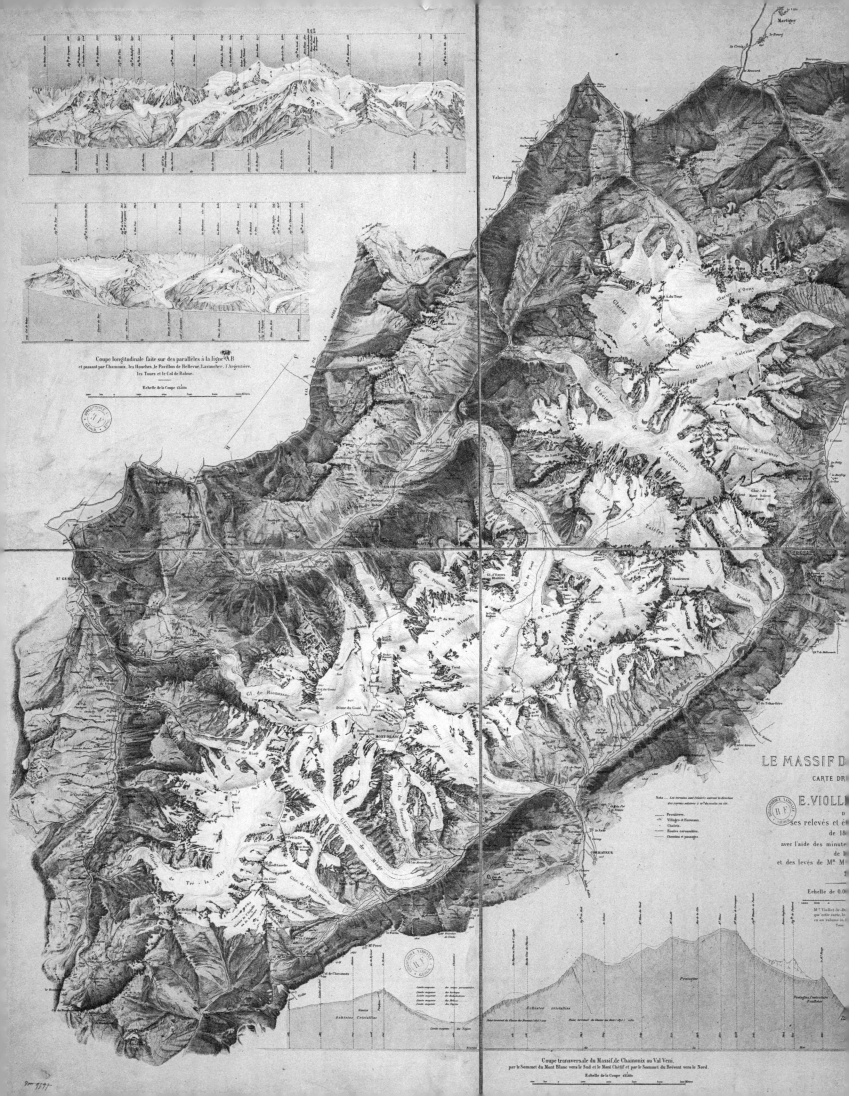

of paper, roughly cast in a sketchbook or drawn in precise detail, surveys have long been used by architects to observe and comprehend the site, its conditions and its boundaries. Some are intended to inspect or to explore, to speculate or to scrutinise. Others are made for different motivations: out of novelty or boredom, for money or even as poetry. A survey might be contingent or idealised, abstract or symbolic, absolute or ephemeral. It might map no other site than the architect's psyche: their references, their interests, or their desire to transform the existing conditions of their world. By its very nature, the survey tends to be incomplete, naïve, subjective, its name even a source of confusion among American colleagues, who mostly prefer 'measured drawing'. And as much as it documents what already exists, the survey is also a site for the imagination. It is not a passive object or record, but an agent and instrument of power. It moves, circulating as a medium of exchange, and it argues, questioning our notion of the architectural site as a place of activity, a place for appropriation, and a place for the formation of identity. It is always, consequently, two things at once: a tool for recording the present and a mode for projecting into a past or future; a way of documenting what is right there in front of our eyes, and a provocation to conjure something new into being.

*Starting*

In this sense the Bellman's Chart is not so different from the drawings made by the first-year architecture students at the Swiss Federal Institute of Technology (ETH) in Zurich, where I teach. As in many schools of architecture, students draw *something* – a room, a piece of furniture, the outline of their body – as a way of beginning to learn the subject. In the case of the ETH, each cohort over five years is tasked with preparing a portion of a 1:100 section that cuts across the city of Zurich, from its northeast to its southwest boundaries.[1] The on-site survey lasts barely a day, but months are spent preparing material and organising access to the interiors of buildings along the section's path. Before undertaking this intensive project, students must also learn how to make a survey. For anyone new to the task, it helps to begin with something familiar; in the case of the first years, this means the HIL, home of the Department of Architecture. Set on a hill on the outskirts of the city, the HIL is a four-storey building from the mid-1970s, a groundscraper wrapped around a garden courtyard, with a forgettable bronze curtain wall.

Eugène-Emmanuel Viollet-le-Duc, Massif du Mont Blanc, map drawn at 1:40,000, 1876. Chromolithography by Georges Erhard, 1175 × 995 mm. Courtesy Département des cartes et plans, Bibliothèque Nationale, Paris

It had snowed in the morning before our survey, with large soft-white flecks falling across Zurich. By late afternoon parts of the campus were inaccessible. Students skipped seminars held in distant buildings, the shuttle bus back to the city showed up less frequently, and the herd of cows that usually grazed on the nearby fields was kept indoors. By evening the snow had turned to sleet and then to rain, washing away the remains of the day's work. But the next day, by lunchtime, a hot sun filled the sky. That afternoon, our first drawing session, the HIL was bathed in light so intense that the people coming and going were reduced to shadows, an effect that flattened the sense of the building, making the idea of recording its every dimension almost impossible. I met the students in the shade of the portico. This was where our sequence would begin, before moving onto the adjacent square, then the interiors directly above, containing the library and materials collection, itself topped by a rooflight. We had no scaffolding and therefore no chance of reaching this final element. Incompleteness, I told them, was fine – this was just a trial run. But it was still important that their work be a momentary snapshot or synthesis of the building and its world: its signage and its structure, the radiators as well as the rubbish, the books, the laptops and the Mr Chips food truck – like me, an English exile – that was closing up for the day.

To make a survey like this you have to measure in a sequence: inside to outside, room to room, corner to corner. You begin by registering the principal dimensions of a space – the perimeter points and the diagonals. You then plot these points on paper to form a geometric outline. After the outline measurements are complete, you start measuring from one point and working around it, aided by rulers, tapes and lasers. As you measure and record the details, you cross-check them against each other and the overall dimensions. Establishing a rough scale or using a key plan is advisable, otherwise the traces of your afternoon will be harder to fit together. Working in tandem also helps: one person measures, another repeats the measurement; one person confirms, another draws.

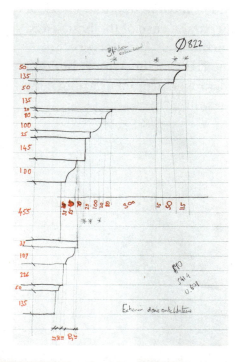
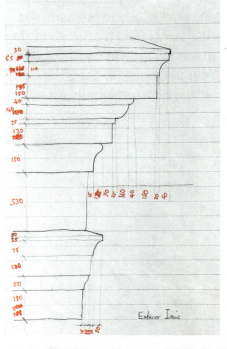

Everyone photographs. One of the challenges in surveying a building of several storeys, like the HIL, is ensuring that the details of each floor line up when overlaid. Various techniques have been developed to help with this: pricking, tracing paper, or CAD layers. Still more difficult, when it comes to preparing the section, is calculating the unseen parts of a building – the thickness of a concrete floor slab, say, or the slope of a tiled roof. To find this, you can use the information you have already recorded in plan and photographed in elevation and take vertical measurements from these known points. If you cannot gain access to the whole of the building, in many cases you can measure one standardised element, like a cladding panel or a pane of glass, and study how the system repeats itself to establish the overall dimensions. Some parts of a facade, such as cornices and mouldings, have to be divided into smaller horizontal and vertical geometries which are then plotted together to record an accurate curved profile. More ornamental details can be sketched separately at a larger scale in section, elevation and maybe even perspective, with their location highlighted on the plan. And since there are invariably limits to what a drawing alone can tell you, a system of symbols, abbreviations and notes is also useful in organising dimensions and details. Once you are back at your desk and away from the site, the exact purpose of a line in pen or pencil is often revealed by these annotations, which give the drawing something substantive, anchoring it in data and facts.

But no matter how much information you include, your survey will never be complete. Like every other form of architectural representation, the survey is both objective and subjective; universal and personal. Standardised practices are necessary for others to understand what is on the page, but at the same time the production of a survey is contingent on the people undertaking the work and the instruments available. For example, a survey might be localised in its measurements (using metric or imperial or archaic systems) but comprehensive in its ambitions (the classification of antique buildings, the study of a whole city). Its level of accuracy hinges not only on whether scaffolding is available to take roof measurements, but also on the time of day (have you eaten?), the weather, who you're working with, your experience and, perhaps less tangibly, what interests you. A survey, then, is both a record of a place and, potently, a register of all the things that inform it. In fact, the drawing depends for its very existence on these variables.

*opposite*
ETH students surveying the HIL Building, ETH Hönggerberg, Zurich, 28 February 2020; David Valinsky, cornice details of St Michael, Berg am Laim, 2020

*below*
William Leybourn, *The Compleat Surveyor*, 1657. Courtesy ETH Library, ETH Zurich

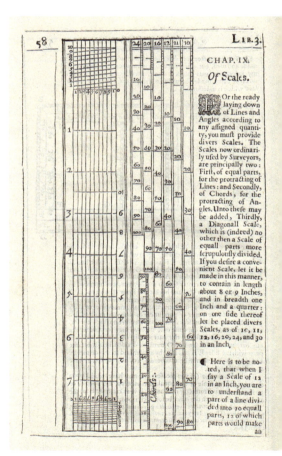

Álvaro Siza, studies for installation for *Sensing Spaces*, Royal Academcy of Arts, London, 2014. Pen and ink, 295×210 mm

*Reference*

And this is where the survey reveals itself as more than a passive object. Though etymologically its origins can be traced to the Latin *supervidere* (*super-*, 'over' + *videre*, 'to see'), the actions involved in making it are perhaps more closely tied to the idea of reference – from the Latin *referre*, meaning to bring back, to register, to record. At its most fundamental level the survey is a record that takes different forms. It can be a simple technique of observation: the documentation of a place, archaeological remains, the condition of a building for sale. But it can also be a technique of control: the production of maps, the administration of property, the declaration of expertise within a particular social group. Or a technique of study: the construction of histories (geological, cultural), the reconstruction of monuments, the production of precedent. Architects need the survey-as-record to provide the certain foundations for building up the precise dimensions for construction they communicate in their working drawings. Archaeologists need a survey as a basis for identifying the precise locations for excavations or proposed reconstructions. In the hands of others – cartographers, tax inspectors, insurance companies, estate agents and many more – the survey becomes the means of establishing the geographic and financial boundaries of modern life. In all of these different ways, it works through the creation of reference. Always with reference to something else – a place, building, a moment in time, units of measurement, a few favourite images, memories – the survey operates as a guarantor of magnitude and distances, surfaces and details.

At the beginning of design, when confronted with the pressure of a blank page, the use of references offers a way in, a starting point. We can see this process play out in a series of drawings Álvaro Siza made while planning his installation for the 2014 *Sensing Spaces* exhibition at London's Royal Academy. In a sketch of his assigned site, the courtyard in front of Burlington House, he depicts his own hand in the bottom-right corner of the sheet, poised over an empty notebook. His hand is present because the work of designing is about to commence. But the loose survey of the courtyard, the outline of its monuments and features, is where Siza has already begun. As he notes in the accompanying catalogue, 'For me, making architecture means starting with what is there'.[2] A kindred spirit might be found in the Irish architect Níall McLaughlin, who has described how he scrutinises architecture through drawings based on his own visits

*below*
Níall McLaughlin, sketchbook, 2018.
Courtesy the architect

*opposite*
Baldassare Peruzzi, plan of the Pantheon, Rome, *c* 1519, Department of Prints and Drawings, Uffizi, Florence

to the building and on photographs. More analytical study than exact record, these 'commonplace sketches' can show a corner of a building, how it was constructed, and how it has weathered over time, all in outlines made in pen. For McLaughlin this drawn analysis – which he describes as a performative act – provides more information than a photograph. In turn it becomes a reference for other current and future projects, to be revisited when a particular question needs to be developed further.

And so, a place becomes a rough survey, sketches and measurements. That draft then becomes a CAD drawing, onto which imagined new places might be overlaid. Or perhaps a place becomes a sketch, the sketch becomes a record drawing, the record drawing becomes a concept, and the concept becomes a new mode of practice. Neither of these contemporary approaches is unique in the history of architecture. Looking back to the sixteenth century, and the initial wave of measured drawings of the monuments of ancient Rome, and notably the Parthenon, we can see how they served at least two interconnected purposes for architects of the time. While the process of surveying gave insight into the details and composition of antique architecture, as a corpus these drawings became a longstanding resource that informed new designs in the Cinquecento.[3] Numerous versions of these drawings exist, and we know that not all of them were made directly on the site. Many were transferred from one sheet to another, by different hands, moving from place to place. These copies show the survey to be not just a singular entity but a whole system for producing and exchanging knowledge. Each copy emphasises something different: construction, function, materiality, decoration, proportion, and in doing so shows us not only what has been lost to the present but also what the individual draughtsman considered worthy of recording.

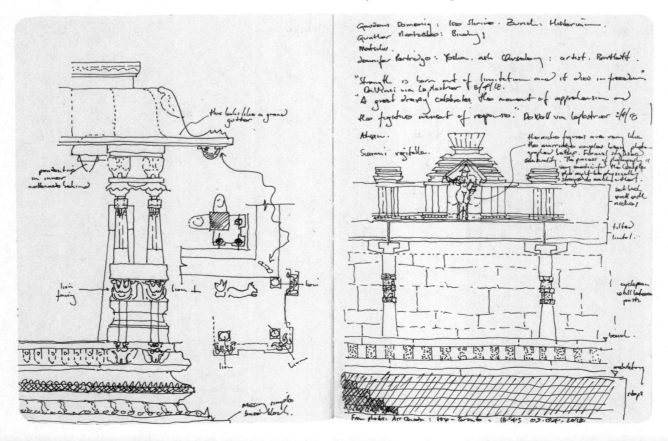

Surveys of the existing fabric of the Baths of Diocletian, made around the same time, reveal not only individual conceptions of antique architecture but also widely varying systems of measurement and styles of drawing. Early on, in 1514–15, Raphael had attempted to codify the plan, section and elevation as the three drawing techniques appropriate for surveying Roman monuments.[4] But in reality, the objectivity of these methods was never flawless. Donato Bramante, measuring in Roman *palmi*, drew a plan of the existing structure to explore how a single structural element such as a pier could articulate four adjoining spaces and simultaneously support vaulting and a roof (a problem he continually returned to in his work). Andrea Palladio, on the other hand, surveyed the complex with measurements taken in his local *piedi vicentini*, which were then translated into a series of reconstructed plans, sections and perspectives with reinterpreted courtyards and elements like the serliana added to the ruined complex. Palladio used theoretical ideas relating to the symmetry, proportion and order of antique architecture to reconstruct the past through drawings, even when only a small portion of that past remained visible in the present. This study of the antique, through comparison, verification and idealised restoration, helped him to create a typology of forms – readymade components that could be expanded or combined in his own contemporary designs for houses, churches or farms.[5]

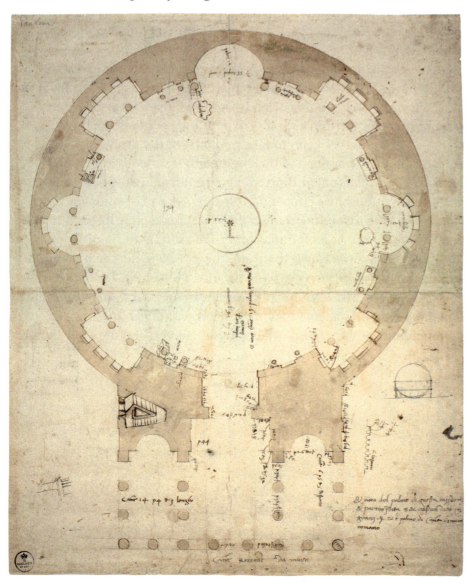

Ephraim Chambers, 'Table of Surveying' from the *Cyclopaedia*, 1728. Courtesy University of Wisconsin-Madison Libraries

*Origins*

'Surveyor', 'Architect' – both were synonymous in eighteenth-century England, when architecture was not yet a profession defined by a body of expert knowledge, but was at least recognisable in its activities. *The Builders' Dictionary* of 1734 determined that the title 'architect' could be used as a kind of shorthand for 'the Surveyor or Superintendent of an Edifice',[6] an assertion affirmed by Samuel Johnson's *Dictionary of the English Language* of 1755. In France, too, both surveyor and architect were responsible for measuring a site and supervising the construction of a building.[7] The title of 'surveyor' went further back, to the early Middle Ages, and described a high-ranking official appointed by the Church or the king to oversee the construction of a building or, equally, the administration of an estate or an institutional body such as the navy. In the construction of the great medieval cathedrals, which could span hundreds of years, the day-to-day tasks of surveying involved not only measuring and certifying new construction work but also monitoring the existing fabric for maintenance and repair.[8] In the Enlightenment this role and the title of 'surveyor' would migrate beyond the Church and State to secular institutions. For instance, James 'Athenian' Stuart held the office of surveyor at Greenwich Hospital from 1758 until his death, while John Soane was surveyor to the Bank of England, overseeing all building works – maintenance and repairs, alterations and additions – at the sprawling City of London complex for 45 years, from 1788 to 1833.

While the making of surveys is fundamental to the making of architecture, the profession has often tried to distance itself from the title 'surveyor'. We see this already in the 1830s, in the construction boom fuelled by Britain's rapidly expanding economy. As the market flooded with builders keen to take on many of the architect's tasks in society, the emergence of the engineer began to encroach on the architect's intellectual authority. Squeezed from two sides, architects tried to shed their less congenial roles in order to establish a clear boundary for a discipline that could be defined solely by artistic and intellectual aims. At its foundation in 1834 the Institute of British Architects (later the Royal Institute, the RIBA) made the disciplinary separation between surveyor and architect absolute. The move was not without its critics. In his influential *Architectural Magazine*, John Claudius Loudon insisted that 'measuring, valuing and estimating [are] as much part of the architect's profession as the making of designs'.[9]

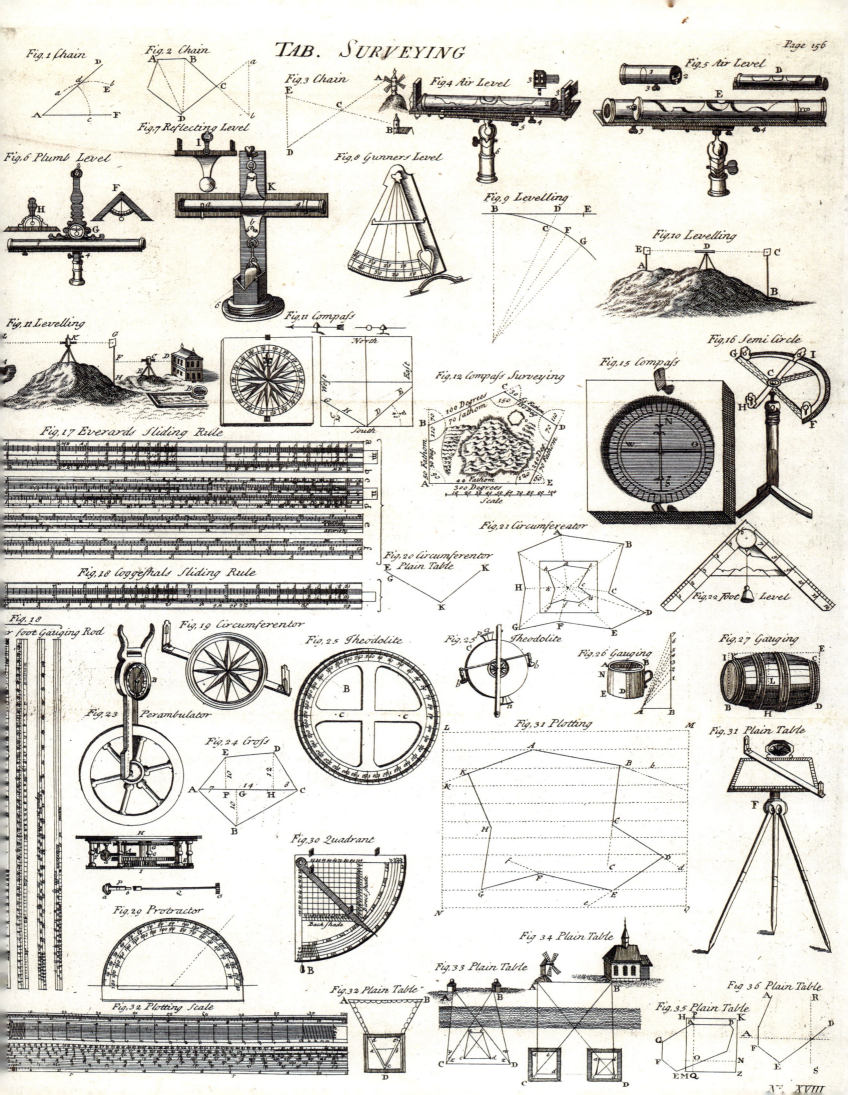

And in practice, notwithstanding the institute's decree, the work of architects remained varied through the nineteenth century, with many relying on surveying (leases, estates and measuring materials) to provide a consistent income alongside the design of new buildings.

In parallel, with the increasing specialisation that accompanied modern industrialisation, both in the field and in the city, the task of 'surveying' expanded beyond its already loose boundaries and took on further nuances, each signalled by an explanatory prefix. Land surveyors, for instance, mapped and measured existing buildings, estimated and supervised repairs; city surveyors worked at a greater scale, plotting the property and administrative boundaries of urban areas; quantity surveyors calculated the materials and labour required for construction. Towards the end of the nineteenth century, the *Architectural Dictionary* described how the survey entailed both making working drawings *and* giving directions on the repair and execution of construction.[10] In other words, the agency of the survey was unclear. Was it related to the objective tasks of inspection and maintenance, or was it an essential part of formulating an individual response to a design brief? Could it in fact be both?

### Projection

Subjectivity and the self are bound into the act of making a survey, as we see when we look back at the survey of the HIL, the one we made earlier with the ETH students. Where are we? Are we far from or close to the site? Have we captured it all on the page? Not all of it, evidently, because we're missing some of the dimensions of the library's rooflight, and we never recorded the texture of a heavily worn carpet or the pile of student work that someone cleared away before the survey was made. Which elements of the facade are original? And what about the steel columns hidden in the wall, which the structural engineer had forgotten all about, even though he had put them there himself only eight years before?[11] When we were measuring, did we stop at the suspended ceiling? Or did we push up a tile or two and crane our heads into the black box to inspect the ductwork and wiring? Let's be honest with ourselves: only those parts we find interesting or useful make it into our drawing. The limits of the drawing are the limits of our record and therefore of our world. But returning to my first question – where are we? We are never very far from the site. In fact, it is in the survey itself that we can most clearly see the multiple sites of architecture, its production and subsequent mediation: the building, the studio, the library, the notebook, the self. Think about those Cinquecento architects, using the drawings of the Pantheon and the Baths of Diocletian – both their accurate observations *and* their mistakes – as a basis for creative reconstruction. Modern archaeology casts doubt on the existence of certain elements used to support conjectural reconstructions. But whether or not they really existed is of secondary importance: what matters more is that the survey forms a set of references and inscriptions – pre-constructed images of our world that are then used as projections for the future.

Never simply a means of retrospection, the subjective survey becomes a vital technique for exploring new ways of thinking about the built environment and society at large. We see this in the work of the Italian architect Adolfo Natalini, who in the late 1960s pushed the agency of the survey to its limits, using it to offer his own distinctive vision for the future. For Natalini, a founding member of the Italian radical collective Superstudio, the Continuous Monument was a critique of the technological determinism of the postwar period. Beginning with a single, endlessly replicable unit – a blank white frame – the structure aggregates into a three-dimensional grid, growing in line with the global population until it occupies all optimal habitats in the world. A sketchbook from the summer of 1969 shows the nucleus of the megastructure taking shape in Florence before cutting across Rome, Vicenza, Athens, the Taj Mahal. It even travels through time, reaching a still extant Crystal Palace. Natalini always begins with something known, a familiar building for the Continuous Monument to latch onto. On one page, the visual grid of perspective renders the caryatid porch of the Erechtheion in Athens into a module measuring five squares wide by two deep, repeated ad infinitum. On another sheet, the Palazzo Chiericati in Vicenza forms the central linking element between two wings of the monument, with the *all'antica* proportions of Palladio's facade defining the module of the monument's three-dimensional grid. On the following page, the Palazzo Pitti in Florence is given a three-storey extension, a block that envelopes the building's massing with a new structure. In every instance, the proportions of the existing building are replicated by the new structure, ultimately producing an architecture that is both monumental and blank, unable to speak but forced to perform. Each time, the logic of the perspective abolishes the distance between the viewer and the imagined scene, drawing the autonomous world confronting the individual into the eye, as Erwin Panofsky

*overleaf*
Adolfo Natalini, Sketchbook 12
(The Continuous Monument), 1969–70.
Pen and ink on thin wove paper,
340 × 275 mm

FACCIATA
PALAZZO CHIERICATI / VICENZA
1550

ATENE / ERETEION
RESTAURO DELLA LOGGIA DELLE CARIATIDI
20.7.69

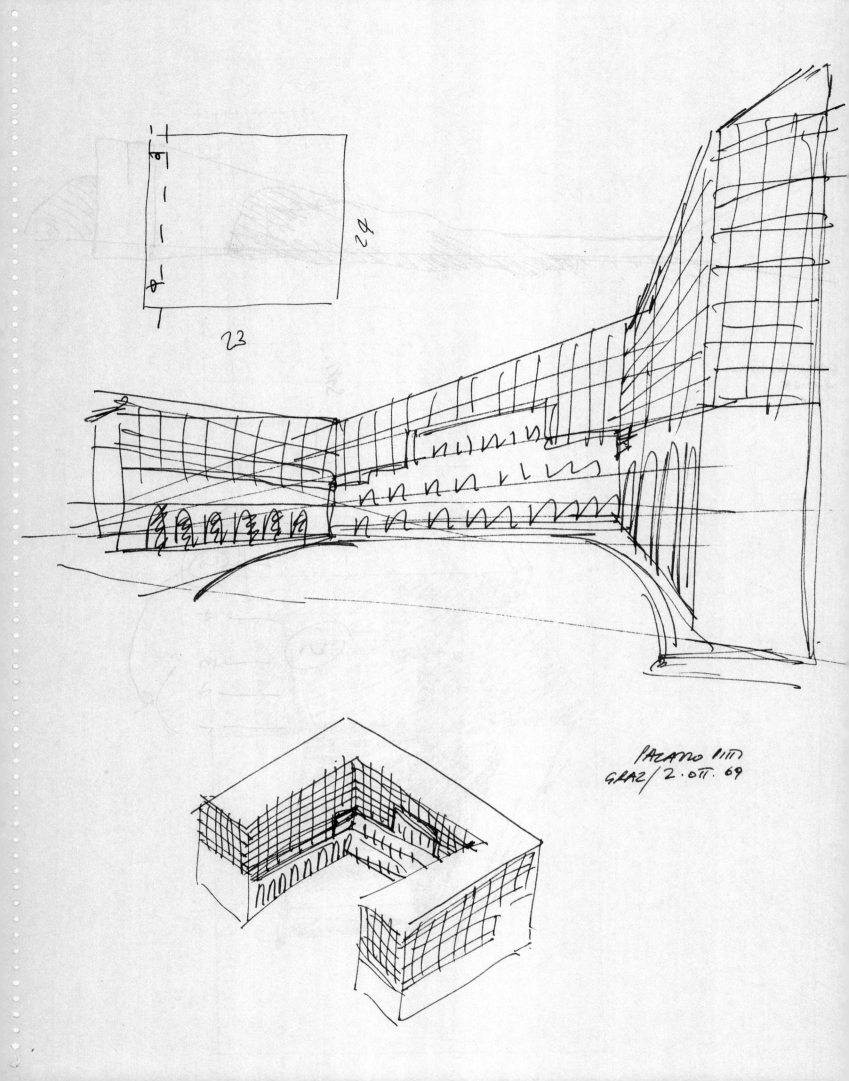

describes it.[12] By beginning with a loose survey of recognisable architecture Natalini embeds his creative vision of the future within the politics and form of the existing built environment. A survey can ground the most radical of ideas in reality.

But the survey can be a creative tool even when there is a physical project to bring to site. Rather than being separate, a mere prelude, the act of making the survey can merge with the act of design. This simultaneity is exemplified by the projects of the Italian architect Alberto Ponis, best known for the hundreds of holiday homes he has built in Sardinia since the mid-1960s. Before he moved to the island, Ponis began his career working for Ernö Goldfinger and Denys Lasdun in London in the 1950s and early 1960s. The sites were largely flat, the projects unrelentingly rational. By contrast, the landscape of Sardinia is rough, undulating, geologically rich and complex; the island sits, along with Corsica, on its own tectonic microplate. For Ponis, this called for work that could 'attach [itself] fully to the earth'.[13] After designing a prototype house for a tourist development at Palau in the north, Ponis began work on a path for a yacht club at nearby Punta Sardegna. From May to the end of June 1965, he and a young stonemason spent mornings walking the site, tracing the landscape with taut string and wooden markers and then recording those points on paper. Independently, Ponis also sketched particular moments where he knew the path needed to bridge a gap or pass through a boulder field.

Back in the office and out of the midday sun, he transcribed this work onto an overall plan of the site. There was no land surveyor on the island, and no instruments capable of making accurate recordings, so Ponis based his survey on military maps and known reference points: a jetty, the beach and prominent rock formations. On the plan the path is marked in orange. It cuts across the landscape from the yacht club to a sandy beach. Black lines drawn onto the orange path show us where gaps have been bridged or stones removed to allow the route to pass. The black-inked landscape of the site is the setting, drawn expressively like a painter's preparatory sketch. Along the path the natural profiles of certain stones allow views to one destination or another, while at other moments the serpentine route twists sharply to avoid particular rocks, bending to form blind spots from the jetty and the beach. The plan shows us a landscape that is cut and displaced to make this path. At the same time, the geology has agency, affecting how humans interact with this altogether new terrain. It is from this survey that the architecture emerges. As Ponis

27

Alberto Ponis, Yacht Club Path, 1965. Coloured inks over print base on yellow paper, 365 × 1007 mm

has said of his houses, they are developed 'around a rock or sequence of rocks. The rock is like the light or fire in the centre of a tent, and all the architectural volumes then start to define themselves by fanning around it. In this sense, it is always the site that makes the design.'[14] In designing forms and shapes that are not 'in any way gratuitous but instead almost inevitable', Ponis has realised an architecture that is united with its landscape, so much so that if one were to now survey the island, parts of the architecture would be inseparable from the terrain, and vice versa.[15]

Yet even the most predetermined architecture requires specific techniques and tools to be understood as such. Architects use a number of approaches to make a single survey, which not only allows us to check our work (after all, the goal here is accuracy), but also affords a layered understanding of the place we are studying, and reminds us that we are never really outside our site. In the case of the yacht club path, and with the trust of his client, who was also on site and knew the area well, Ponis relied on old maps (historical references); his own curiosity about the terrain (personal references); and the help of a local stonemason (an expert). He draws – first with string as he walks, performing the site so that the survey is not only on paper but embodied; and then by transferring all of these physical and remembered details onto a sheet of paper.

Thinking about this methodology, the American historian of urbanism Kevin Lynch has identified three different types of making surveys, each distinguished by its measurements in relation to the site. First, the body: short distances can be gauged by pacing up, down and across, although, as Lynch notes, the surveyor needs to know the length of their gait, 'having counted, on several occasions, the number

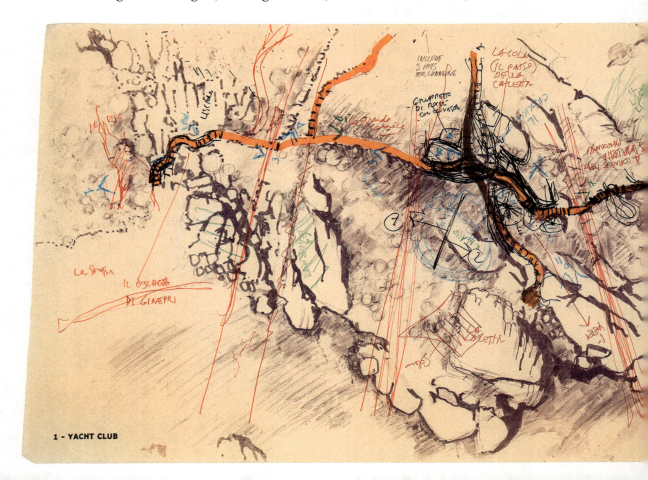

1 - YACHT CLUB

of strides [they] use to cover a measured course'.[16] Second, the mind: longer distances can be estimated by eye. Objects and features in the landscape – telephone poles, football fields – can be observed and 'chains of these images ... mentally overlaid on the ground before one another'.[17] The final method of making surveys is by using tools. While these can be as basic as chalk or Alberto Ponis's string, they can also be as complicated as the details they are used to describe. The cymograph is one example: invented in 1842 by the engineer and mathematician Robert Willis, it was intended to simplify the task of measuring mouldings in the field, but the device itself was almost impossible to use.[18] At the opposite end of the scale, Lynch refers to Gunter's chain, designed in 1620 by the English clergyman and mathematician Edmund Gunter and still used in various forms today. An extremely simple device – a 66ft (20.1m) chain divided into 100 links – it nevertheless allows for a fair degree of accuracy. (You may also know this unit as the length of a cricket pitch.) Assisted by a chainman, a surveyor places markers at the boundaries and other significant points of a site. From one marker to another, the site is measured in lengths of the chain (pulled taut, the ends pegged with marker pins). Chain, chainman and surveyor march across the field in a process called 'ranging', or in the US, 'chaining', which makes it easy to quantify land for legal and commercial purposes. Invented in the early years of the English colonisation of America (in fact the same year the *Mayflower* sailed from Plymouth), Gunter's chain would become an instrument of colonial dispossession, facilitating the land grants of westward expansion that erased indigenous places and granted the white European settlers exclusive rights to a specific portion of the earth, which would be claimed as private property, fenced off, cleared and cultivated.[19]

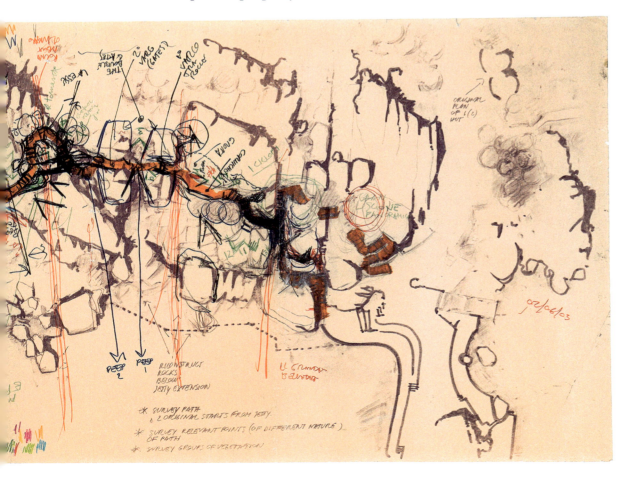

William Leybourn, *The Compleat Surveyor*, 1657. Courtesy ETH Library, ETH Zurich

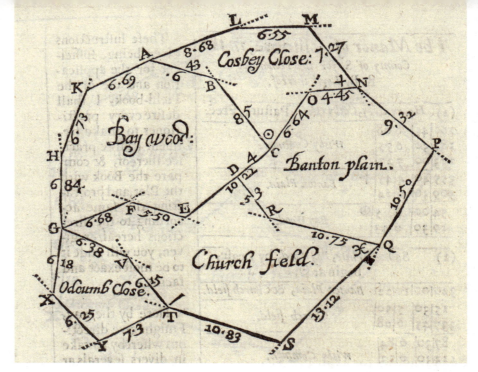

*Boundaries*

Not purely a vehicle for enforcing western expansionism, the survey also contributed to a reverse flow of knowledge about other cultures, particularly following the establishment of architectural institutions. A case in point is the model of a Chinese Chemist's House and Shop exhibited at a meeting of the RIBA in 1847.[20] The model had been produced for a prominent London pharmacist who was keen to know more about one of his Guangzhou counterparts in the wake of the First Opium War (1839–42).[21] Made by local craftsmen, it conveyed key information about the building in relation to the local climate and social habits.[22] Though its formal expression – derived from 'the tents of their herdsmen-ancestors' – met with the condescension typical of the time, the architectural press used this example to make a broader point regarding the enduring power of building forms, noting their persistence in contemporary London, where even 'ugly' buildings were copied, and every repetition further spoiled public taste.[23] In other words, the survey of a traditional Chinese pharmacy allowed for a new understanding of prevailing conditions in nineteenth-century Britain.

Parallel to this strand of ethnographic curiosity was a growing interest in non-European architecture, as an antidote to the ills of modern industrialisation. While Gottfried Semper's pseudo-ethnographic analysis of the 'Caribbean Hut' at the Great Exhibition of 1851 is well known, many others were documenting traditional buildings on study trips to all corners of the world. Drawing on a methodology of classification that was being developed in the sciences, publications like James Fergusson's study of Vijayapura (1859) or Hermann Frobenius's *Afrikanische Bautypen* (1894) provided accounts of indigenous architecture, substantiated by surveys. In Fergusson's case, these surveys were photographic copies of drawings made by local draughtsmen or views made with the help of a new technology, the camera lucida.[24] A devotee of accuracy, Fergusson was critical of the imprecise work of a previous generation of travellers in India, among them Thomas Daniel and William Hodges. Confident in his own abilities, he referred to his 'picturesque' illustrations as 'the most perfect delineations of Indian Architecture' available to the public.[25] Frobenius's work took a more tectonic emphasis in its study of traditional African building types described in measured drawings.[26] Influenced by ethnographic studies, the analysis of the 'periphery' beyond Europe helped to redefine conceptions of architecture at its 'centre', fuelling contemporary debates on European architectural practice.[27]

The survey, then, represents the very fine line between gaining understanding and gaining control. At worst, some of this architectural research, especially by the early twentieth century, was being used to promote reductive, nationalist agendas – if not explicitly, then tacitly. At its best, however, the survey is a method for asking questions about the architecture in front of us, the contexts it sits within, and our relationship to the built environment. The examples that follow present six very different approaches to the survey. The protagonists are, admittedly, among the most well known in the western canon of architecture, selected not only for the role the survey plays in their individual practice, but also for the reverberations of their uses of the survey into further generations. The long nineteenth century figures strongly as a moment when the survey was used by architects to first gain control and then reinforce their position in society as a whole. By making a survey, an architect could gain knowledge of the past (eg archaeological remains), record the present (eg the progress of construction on site), or from close analysis offer new directions for modern life. In each case the architect is using multiple techniques to make a survey, and over the course of their practice their reasons for making surveys change in line with their shifting objectives or circumstances. The aim here is not to suggest one definitive approach, but instead to show the possibilities of the survey – its conditions, its goals, and ultimately its effects on architecture as we understand it today.

*Surveys in Practice*

*John Soane: The Construction Site*

Architectural education in Europe has for centuries privileged the tacit knowledge embodied in making a survey. From 1769, students at the newly founded Royal Academy (RA) Schools in London would make measured drawings of buildings as an integral part of their training, which was intended to complement their pupillage in an architect's office. Each year would begin with a competition for the best measured drawing, which was awarded the RA's Silver Medal. Accuracy was key: all drawings were checked by one or more of the Academicians – the prominent artists of the day. The subject of the competition was invariably a building located within ten miles of the institution's base. In 1771 students were assigned the 'Front next the Thames of the Royal Academy' (their equivalent of the HIL). As a new student, just turned 18, John Soane (1753–1837) probably laboured with another student to measure the facade, first with rods and a tape before using string and lead strips to gauge the profile of the cornices and mouldings. They moved across the site, making outline drawings on folded sheets that were mounted onto a portable board. While these rough but meticulously annotated working drawings are by Soane, the final drawing is in the hand of Robert Baldwin, a draughtsman who had previously worked for George Dance the Younger, Soane's mentor and a founding member of the Royal Academy. The submission deadline was 1 November 1771, one week after Soane's enrolment. He missed it by a day. But he got his Silver Medal the following year, for a drawing of the Banqueting House at Whitehall. Here, too, Soane seems to have taken all the measurements before commissioning Baldwin to produce a presentation drawing.[28] Similar to the pyramidal scheme of the ateliers at the Beaux-Arts school in Paris, where final drawings were not the work of a single author but of a cohort of hands, this process suggests that the experience gained in making a survey was considered more important than the finished product.

New knowledge can arise from leaving the places you know. After winning the Royal Academy's Gold Medal in November 1776 with a project for a 'Triumphal Bridge', Soane was awarded a royal scholarship that provided for a three-year sojourn in Rome.[29] He would leave for Italy in March 1778 and return in June 1780. From Soane's time abroad we have just over 100 surveys of buildings, mainly in Italy, as well as four sheets of drawings of eighteenth-century

*previous spread*
Soane Office, site progress view, Dulwich Picture Gallery, made to accompany Royal Academy Lecture, 1812. Pencil and coloured washes, watercolour technique, shaded on laid paper, 235 × 165 mm
© Sir John Soane's Museum, London

*below, opposite, and overleaf*
John Soane with Thomas Hardwick, Temple of Minerva Medica, including a section of the Nymphaeum, partial plans and plan, *c* 1778. Pen, sepia washes, pencil, 617 × 455 mm; 562 × 438 mm; 725 × 534 mm © Sir John Soane's Museum, London

bridges in Switzerland. Some are copies of other architects' work rather than measured surveys made by Soane himself; the tell-tale signs include marks showing where he has pricked through the sheets to make transfers, and the use of non-English, region-specific drawing scales. Surviving sketchbooks contain on-site studies of buildings and archaeological remains at Tivoli, Pompeii and of course Rome, where Soane immediately set to 'examining the numerous and estimable remains of Antiquity' when he arrived at the beginning of May 1778.[30] Soon after, he joined forces with a fellow student at the Royal Academy, Thomas Hardwick, who was wealthy enough to fund his own Grand Tour. Through the month of June, the pair moved from one monument to the next, dividing the tasks of measuring and recording equally. An obsession with detail drives their surveys, but the focus is less on the exact intricacies of the orders or ornamental decoration, and more on the overall composition of a building, studied and expressed in plan to clearly record its spatial organisation. Sometimes their desire for exactitude led them down the path of danger. In surveying the so-called Temple of Minerva Medica (actually a ruined nymphaeum), they climbed up the crumbling brick dome to examine its clerestory windows, and leant out

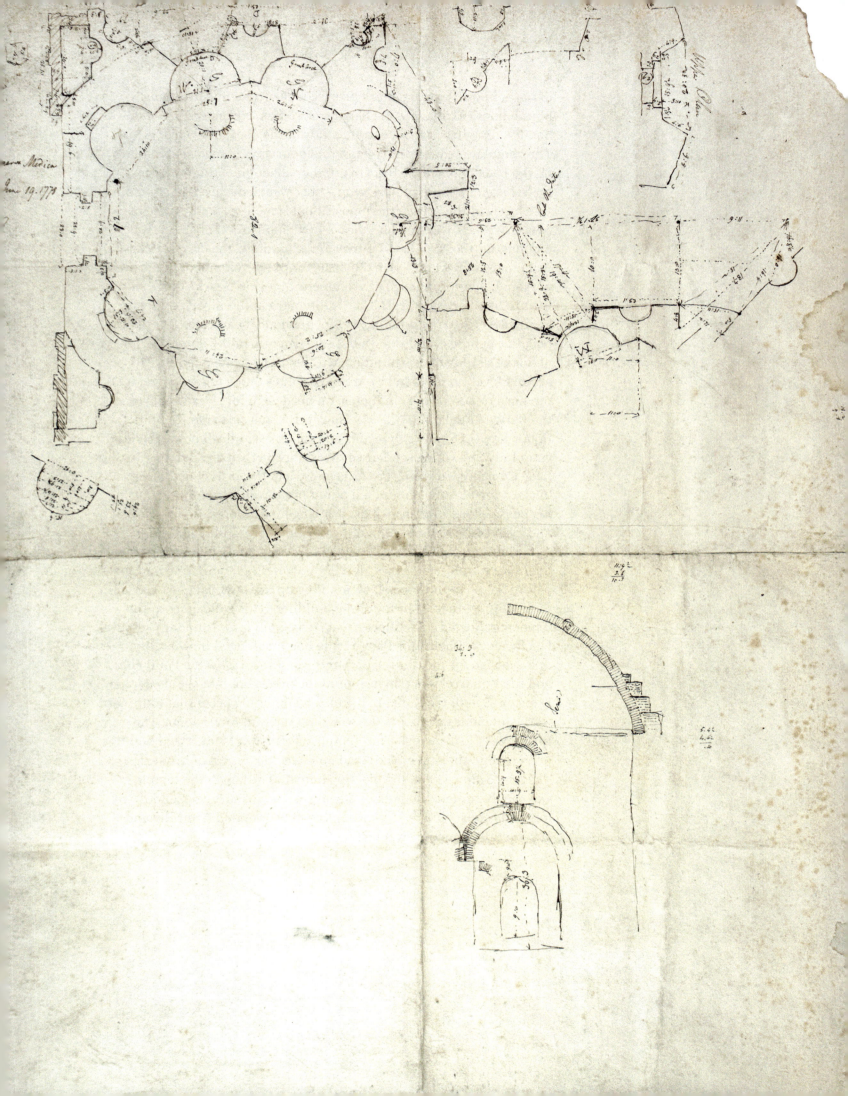

of holes in walls to take more precise measurements, dropping plumb lines to calculate the heights of arches, cornices and windows. Soane's drawings show a careful study of the decagonal structure. The complete sequence of niches and doorways is recorded in plan on the back of one drawing. On another sheet, the building's geometric skeleton, drawn in section – observed, measured, marked out – emerges as the primary compositional structure. Soane's use of pencil overlaid with ink and then a final application of a faint wash emphasises the structure's purity and simplicity, the classical 'first principles' that would form the basis for the development of his own personal, poetic language of architectural forms. Years later, in a lecture he gave as Professor of Architecture at the Royal Academy, Soane described the building as 'uncommonly beautiful ... there is a peculiar lightness and skill in the construction of the dome'.[31] Looking at Soane's study of this building, with its large-scale openings at ground level surmounted by arched lunettes and a top-lit dome, it is not hard to perceive its influence on his design for the rotunda of the Bank of England (1794–95). However, concrete evidence of the importance of Soane's time abroad remains scant. Homeward bound from Italy, the young scholar set his sights on Switzerland, passing Lake Como and crossing the Alps to Zurich. It was during this leg of his journey that the bottom fell out of his travelling trunk, scattering his possessions – his drawings, drawing instruments, books, clothes and even his medals from the Royal Academy – to the four winds.

The Temple of Minerva Medica's allure, and its influence on contemporary architecture, was felt not only in England. Three months before Soane found himself scrambling up its walls, Jacques-Germain Soufflot presented a survey of the building to his colleagues at the Académie Royale d'Architecture in Paris. Soufflot was under pressure. His former collaborator Pierre Patte had challenged the viability of his design for the Church of Sainte-Geneviève (now the Panthéon) and their quarrel was playing out in the press. Soufflot set his nephew, François Soufflot le Romain, the task of obtaining proof that four piers were sufficient to support the weight of the building's dome. The result was the drawing of the Temple of Minerva Medica that Soufflot presented to the assembled Académiciens in support of his design. The proceedings from the meeting note that although the temple was partly ruined, the bulk of the structure had survived, and therefore 'this construction seems suitable to be imitated fruitfully and successfully in many circumstances'.[32]

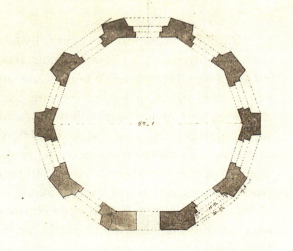

François Soufflot le Romain, Temple of Minerva, Rome, 1778. Black ink and coloured washes, with black pencil detailing on paper, 450 × 550 mm

But if the intention was primarily to prove the fitness of the structure, then why, as Basile Baudez has asked, is the drawing so pictorial and decorative? Whereas Soane's section of the 'temple' is a more abstract, analytical drawing that focuses on measured distances and structure, Soufflot le Romain offers us the image of a building with landscape and pastoral figures. He negates the element of abstraction inherent in the orthographic section by using coloured wash to present a painterly view of the architecture that encompasses deterioration and decay, shadow and depth, vegetation and clouds. In contrast to Soane's and Hardwick's acrobatic clambering over the building, the two figures in the far-left corner of Soufflot le Romain's drawing stand at a remove, poised in front of their drawing boards, not looking at the antique building, but still drawing its picturesque qualities.

In the years following Soane's return to England the pictorial survey would have a clear role to play in his own practice. Soane's pupils were often asked to travel to building sites in pairs and record works under construction as part of their training. During the summer of 1812, when the construction of the Dulwich Picture Gallery was well underway, a younger pupil, George Basevi, made two trips together with the more senior Robert Chantrell, one at the beginning of June, the other at the end. The rough sketches they made were then

pasted into the record book back at the office in Lincoln's Inn Fields. (One sketch by Basevi has an added trompe l'oeil scroll to simulate the effect of a tipped-in plate.) In these drawings we can see certain parts of the complex – the associated mausoleum and almshouses – at an early stage of their construction. Two more drawings show the progress of the bricklayers as they laid the arches of the gallery's central enfilade. Later in the summer three others – George Allen Underwood, John Buxton and George Bailey – travelled to Dulwich to make further records of the site. Their drawings depict the London stock brick structure with its Portland stone dressing and the intricate timber framework of the gallery's innovative octagonal skylights. We see the mixture of trades, the liveliness and messiness as the building emerges from the ground. In the foreground of early drawings, figures work alongside piles of bricks, sand and cement, with sculpted decoration dotted around, ready to be installed. Between the figures and materials is the technical apparatus of the construction site: an array of machines, ladders, sheds and other structures for the fabrication of particular elements. Notably these drawings capture the variety of temporary works implemented by the labourers and their different temporal registers: external scaffolding for the brickwork, internal supports to prop up the brick walls as they are being laid, and high-level platforms to allow access to the skylights and roof. They also show how architectural practice was changing in response to the emergence of the new environmental systems which were installed within the building fabric to support modern notions of comfort. One drawing from July 1812 depicts the service ducts beneath the floor, with their short brick walls to protect the gallery's steam heating pipes (a closed circuit that failed in 1813, when cold water leaked into the pipes of the hot water system). As a corpus, these survey drawings function as a more labour-intensive version of the work-in-progress iPhone snapshots that we take when we visit our buildings on site. They not only show the skeleton of one of Soane's major buildings, but also provide a record of the pace of construction.

When architects travelled, surveying buildings and landscapes, it was not only technical devices but the technical infrastructure of production that fascinated them. On his visit to France and Britain in 1826, Karl Friedrich Schinkel toured not only the cultural sights of London, Edinburgh and Paris, but also ironworks and gasworks. And whereas Soane's Bank of England merits three short sentences in his diary – several curved facades, pointless courtyard (Lothbury Court),

Soane Office, progress view, Dulwich
Picture Gallery, made to accompany
Royal Academy Lecture, 1812.
Pencil and coloured washes, water-
colour technique, shaded on laid paper
© Sir John Soane's Museum, London

but excellent triumphal entrance to the street – an account of the
ironworks and furnaces of Dudley, capital of the Black Country, takes
up a whole page.[33] The notes of his visit on 20 June are accompanied
by a series of sketches that show how Schinkel is interested in every
aspect of the commercial iron trade and its effect on the landscape.
He outlines the whole process of production, from his arrival via the
twelve-foot-wide canal connecting the town with Birmingham, to the
landscape of 'thousands of smoking obelisks' on the horizon.[34] He
visits machinery extracting bituminous coal from thick seams, bring-
ing it to the surface. Moving on to Tipton, a new town caught between
the old and new lines of the Birmingham Canal, Schinkel describes
the Gospel Oaks ironworks in action, with their furnaces, rolling
mills and tin-plating machinery housed in a brick and iron shed – the
brick wobbles under the forces of production, the columns are com-
posite elements, both holding up the building's roof and containing
the water drainage systems. As he leaves Tipton, on the way to the
Wedgwood factories in Newcastle-under-Lyme, Schinkel catches sight
of the ruinous complex of Dudley Castle on a hillside surrounded
by trees. From one side it appears a picturesque ruin; from the other,
Schinkel sees the 'magnificent view' of a limestone hill undermined
with a network of tunnels and quarries extracting and burning the
lime that would be transported around the country to fuel the manu-
facture of mortar or iron, essential components in the production
of modern buildings.

When these industrial building products reached the site,
Soane believed that surveying their construction would give young
architects a greater understanding of the practice of construction.[35]
To illustrate this point he selected four of the Dulwich Picture Gallery
drawings to include in his twelfth lecture to students at the Royal
Academy Schools. These reproductions are enlarged in size, shown
in greater detail than the originals, and set within dark ink borders
on high-quality paper. While they clearly demonstrate the abilities
of his pupils, Soane was using them in this context to argue for a particular pedagogical approach. This 'mode of study', which involved
not only drawing designs for buildings but recording the process
of their construction in real time, encouraged the student to 'observe
and treasure up in his mind a variety of forms and ideas that the
same buildings when finished would not convey'.[36] In other words,
drawing the site in action was a way of recording future lessons
for oneself – lessons not just about the design of a building but

about the organisational skills and technical understanding that an architect needed to develop alongside his artistic abilities. Individually, each of these snapshots is its own survey, but taken collectively they add to a complex understanding of architecture's production. Through Soane's presentation, the four drawings are transformed from office references to tools for projecting honed messages – statements of intent. This shift of intention is revealing. It shows us that the original reasons for making a survey are not always the reasons why we return to it later. A survey need not only be a representation of the world, but can also be a re-presentation of it to a new audience.

*C R Cockerell: The Survey of Antiquity*

A drawing of the Parthenon by William Gell from 1801 shows a man on a ladder climbing to the level of the temple's entablature. That man is Giovanni Battista Lusieri, a Neapolitan artist who worked as Lord Elgin's draughtsman and organised the removal of the Parthenon marbles. Elgin appears to have had permission from Greece's Ottoman rulers to survey the site, in an official decree outlining how draughtsmen and artists like Gell could freely enter the Acropolis, draw and model with plaster, erect scaffolding and excavate foundations. Interpreting that as authorisation to also plunder works of art,[37] Elgin made off with around half of the surviving Parthenon sculptures over the course of the following decade. By the time Charles Robert Cockerell (1788–1863) arrived in Athens in 1810, only a few crates remained to be shipped. But the ladder was still there, it seems: the back of one of the sheets in Cockerell's survey of the Parthenon bears the scant notation 'Ladder of Mr Lusieri'.[38]

Cockerell spent the winter of 1810–11 in a house with a garden full of orange trees and a single palm. He used this time to draw material on and around the Acropolis, studying the buildings very closely, something few western Europeans had been able to do for several decades. For this task, ladders were useful, but scaffolding was even better, providing a more stable platform for observation. The following year, on the back of a letter to Robert Smirke, in whose office he had trained, Cockerell drew an elevation of one of the Parthenon's columns – the first documentation of the phenomenon of entasis, the slight convex curve swelling introduced in the centre of the column to correct the visual illusion of concavity.[39] He told Smirke that if he had been able to work with 'a couple of English carpenters', highly skilled in measuring lengths, angles or curves, it would have added greater accuracy and precision to his survey, reinforcing his observation.[40]

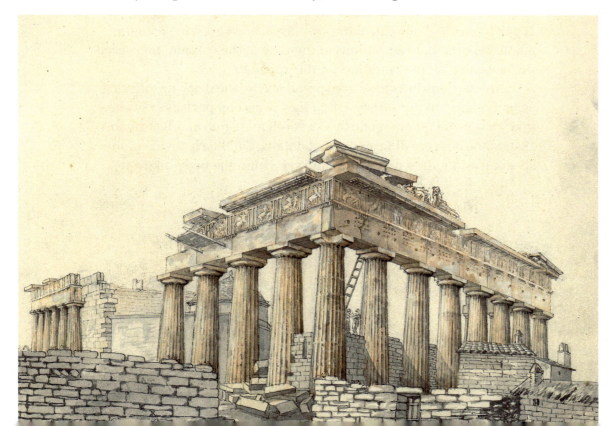

*previous spread*
Carl Haller von Hallerstein, *Charles Robert Cockerell drawing in Eleusis*, July 1811; William Gell, Parthenon, 1811. Pen and ink with brown and black ink wash, 239×338 mm © Trustees of the British Museum

Later engraved and published in Peter Oluf Brøndsted's *Reisen und Untersuchungen in Griechenland* (Travels and Studies in Greece, 1830), Cockerell's drawing of the Parthenon shows us how the survey can first record, then crystallise knowledge. Brøndsted, a Danish archaeologist, was in the circle of international travellers whose 'journey to the Orient' overlapped with Cockerell's. During his time in Athens, Cockerell also befriended Carl Haller von Hallerstein (architect-archaeologist), Count Otto Magnus Baron von Stackelberg (archaeologist, painter), Jakob Linckh (landscape painter) and Louis-François Sebastien Fauvel (French consul and eager collector of antiquities), among others. In the port of Piraeus, he serenaded Lord Byron aboard his ship, and drank a glass of port with him as they discussed the latest military skirmishes off Corfu.[41]

Brøndsted noted that the 'precise and clear representation' of Cockerell's plan, based on his on-site investigations, had turned up details markedly different from earlier surveys of the Parthenon.[42] Notably, Cockerell's study of the marble floor – 'a previously neglected but curious feature' – became a register to uncover and reconstruct the building.[43] Made from three separate sheets of paper glued together, the original drawing captures the extent of the outer colonnade of the temple and everything inside it. Within an outline of ink, two types of wash are used to mediate between the condition of the monument as Cockerell found it and his tentative restoration. An overcast-grey wash marks the columns and walls in situ, with a lighter grey variation noting columns whose remains are presumably fragmentary or partial. A pink-orange ochre wash indicates those parts that are absent but have been deduced by experience and observation. The shades of this wash vary across a spectrum to show the absent, the inferred and the incomplete. In the centre of the plan is the outline of a fifteenth-century mosque, rotated obliquely to the plan of the temple in order to face the Ka'bah in Mecca. At the bottom right of the sheet the pink-orange section of a moulding (plinth and torus) is partly overlaid onto the dark-grey circle of a surviving column; a note reports that excavations at the base of the column uncovered the moulding on the outer face of the upper step.

Annotations like these are spread across the drawing, offering a commentary to the survey. Often they draw comparisons between this survey and others made by Cockerell at Aegina and Bassae in 1811. Some observe differences and details. On the right side of the sheet an annotation marked 'B' and set within the two pink-orange jambs of the door notes: 'These architraves are undoubtedly modern they are well built of stones which have served other purposes'. Other observations are based on Cockerell's study of the damage caused by an explosion in 1687, when the Parthenon was used as a gunpowder store during the war between the Ottoman Empire and the Republic of Venice. Structurally, Cockerell noted, the side walls of the peristyle were reinforced by the cross-braced shear walls and the columns, 'forming a great resistance' to the explosion. Internally, however, the columns were weakened by the added structural requirements of the building lengthwise, so they 'yielded to the impetus of the explosion more easily'. The study of the patina and condition of materials also helped Cockerell make new observations about the building. A well-worn portion of the pavement suggested the presence of ancient doors, which Cockerell indicated by scratching or rubbing the surface of the paper to leave an absent mark. Other conspicuous absences include the residue of the Byzantine church, Theotokos

Charles Robert Cockerell, annotated plan of the Parthenon (overleaf) with verso detail of Aegina marbles (below) 1813. Pen and black ink with pencil and grey and orange wash, 820 × 480 mm

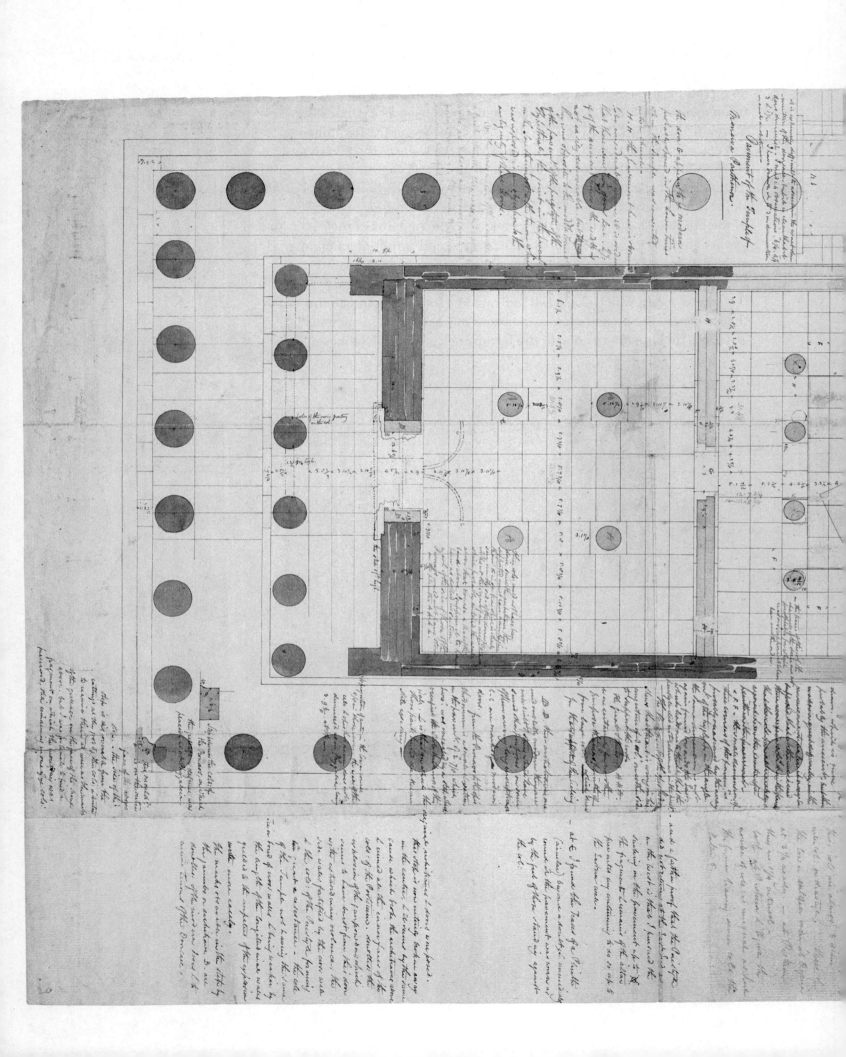

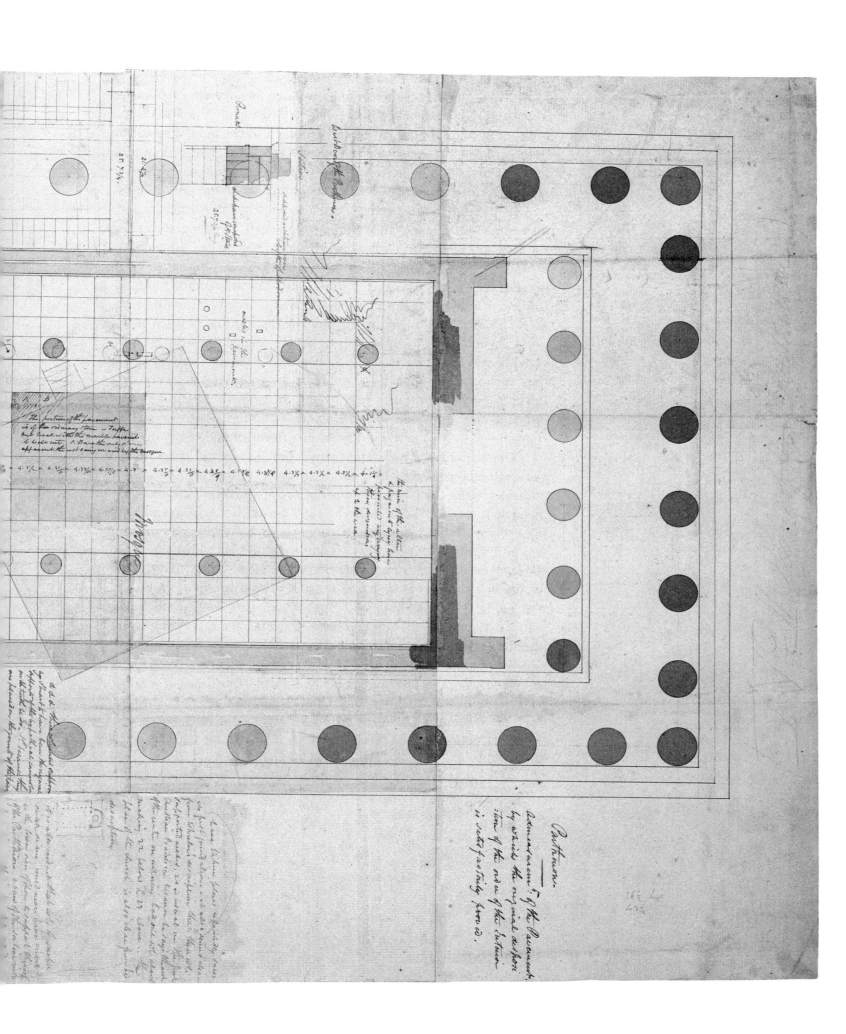

Atheniotissa, which features in a caveat appended to the top of the drawing: the ruin of the altar lying inside the building 'prevented my carrying these dimensions up to the wall'.

In order to make sense of the building, its surviving structure and accumulated debris, Cockerell relies on a grid. A line reads: 'Admeasurement of the Pavement, by which the original disposition of the order of the interior is satisfactorily proved'. We see how a register of points and lines structure the drawing. Points mark the centres of the found and the imagined columns, while the grid of lines depicts the individual paving slabs, arranged in three different series according to the spaces they configure: the central space, the cella; the treasury behind it; and the north wall at the rear of the temple. Distances are measured across the floor, between columns and walls, and between individual paving slabs. The separation of the building into slabs allows Cockerell to metabolise its remains, turning a series of physical things into a geometric inscription, a series of data points held on the sheet. This sheet becomes a mobile storage unit, capable of recording a part of Athens, which is then transferred from the drawing to the engraving, and from the engraving to wherever the book travels, first physically, then through print media – a process that continues now with the drawing photographed and digitally reproduced in the book you are holding in your hand.

The Napoleonic Wars made travel much more difficult for the generation of architects that followed Soane. France and Italy were off limits to the British, but a tour of Greece and Asia Minor was still possible if you had money and the right connections. Cockerell's father knew Lord Elgin's first private secretary, William Hamilton, and pulled some strings to get his son a position as a king's messenger. Cockerell sailed from Plymouth on the *Black Joke* with despatches for the British fleets at Cadiz, Malta and Constantinople, which he reached by the end of May 1810.[44] After spending the summer in the Ottoman capital, Cockerell and his new friend, the Liverpool-based architect John Foster, booked passage for Athens. Setting out in mid-September, they travelled via the ruins of Troy (where, in homage to Achilles, Cockerell stripped naked and ran three times around the alleged tomb of Patroclus), Thessaloniki and the Cyclades. At Andros the crew of their Greek merchantman ransacked their baggage, so they were obliged to change ships. On another island, Cockerell's Skye terrier, Fop, fell into a well and had to be rescued. It was then Foster's turn to have an accident when they landed on the sacred island of Delos – birthplace of Apollo and Artemis – and they were forced to stay put for a while. Since there was nothing to eat on Delos – an English frigate had bought up all the food supplies a few days before – they sent to a nearby island for a goat, which they slaughtered and roasted within the sanctuary of Apollo. Cockerell devoted the enforced stay to 'sketching and measuring everything I could see in the way of architectural remains'.[45] Not content with what he could see on the surface, he directed local men to begin excavating the Temple of the Delians. From this he was able to make out the remains of the columns and prepare a reconstructed plan. Cockerell would develop a taste for excavation after this first dig. The direct examination of the archaeological site helped him to understand fundamental details of the buildings he was surveying, allowing for more accurate reconstructions of their original purpose. As with a new construction site, the efficient organisation of men and machinery, materials and money was key to the success of the excavation – something Cockerell found much harder to achieve than Soane did back home. His travelogue describes his 'greatest pother' with the local labourers, who could 'be uncommonly insolent when there is no janissary to keep them in order'.[46]

On other occasions, Cockerell's approach to measuring and surveying yielded remarkable discoveries. On the back of the Parthenon survey is another drawing, a proposed reconstruction of the west pediment at the Temple of Aphaia on Aegina, dating from the fifth century BCE. Cockerell and Foster had gone there in May 1811, accompanied by their friends Carl Haller von Hallerstein and Jakob Linckh. The group 'set three men to dig and turn over stones that were interesting to our measurements'.[47] Working at a pace that would horrify contemporary archaeologists, they cleared the site of silt and rubble. Organising the temple as a building site allowed them to better understand the tectonic character and proportional relationships of the individual parts to the monument as a whole. Cockerell noted that by the end of a few days' study, the Anglo-German expedition had examined all that was 'necessary for a complete architectural analysis and restoration'. But meanwhile, 'a startling incident had occurred, which wrought us all to the highest pitch of excitement. On the second day, one of the excavators, working in the interior portico, struck on a piece of Parian marble...'[48] That piece of marble would turn out to be a fragment of an extraordinary set of pedimental sculptures that formed a transitional style between

Charles Robert Cockerell, Athens framed by panoramic views, 1816. Etching, 330×470 mm

the archaic and the classical. Digging deeper, the excavators also found limestone faced with stucco, richly painted with bright colours – evidence that polychromy was integral to Greek architecture from the start, in contrast to the prevailing view of its almost abstract purity.

As the pedimental sculptures were removed from the earth, they were measured and drawn with careful precision.[49] The islanders begged them to 'desist from their operations, for heaven only knew what misfortunes might not fall'. Cockerell discounted 'such a rubbishy pretense of superstitious fear' as 'obviously a mere excuse to extort money'. The Northern Europeans had their own, more effective negotiating tactic, which was to ship the sculptures back to Athens under cover of darkness: 'The marbles being gone, the primates came to be easier to deal with. We completed our bargain with them to pay 800 piastres for the antiquities we had found...' In Athens, the marbles were restored and prepared for sale. The treasure was now valued at the 'monstrous figure' of 6,000 to 8,000 Italian Napoleonic lira and was 'not to be divided. It is a collection which a king or great nobleman ... should spare no effort to secure; for it would be a school of art as well as an ornament to any country.'[50] The following year, the marbles were sold to Haller's patron, the Crown Prince of Bavaria, soon to be Ludwig I, and are now on display in the Glyptothek in Munich.

Collections of this kind were installed in newly formed museums of Europe. Although acquired problematically, they could be said to have democratised the essence of the Grand Tour, offering even those of modest means the opportunity to experience the remains of antiquity. Going to the British Museum, the eventual resting place of the Elgin marbles, we see the indelible imprint of Cockerell in the entasis of the columns of the south portico, designed by his former employer Robert Smirke, and in the polychromy of the decorative scheme for the entrance hall, designed by Smirke's son Sydney. Through his work, Cockerell reinvigorated the Greek Revival, injecting it with a greater playfulness and freedom of interpretation. Many of his buildings still stand today, among them the Ashmolean Museum in Oxford, with its borrowings from the Temple at Aphaia; St George's Hall in Liverpool, with the balconies of the concert hall carried on caryatids; and the fragmentary National Monument of Scotland – just 12 columns of a projected full-scale replica of the Parthenon on top of Calton Hill in Edinburgh, the 'Athens of the North'.

## Hippolyte Lebas, Henri Labrouste: The Envoi de Rome

Rather than being set in stone, perceptions of classical architecture have always remained remarkably fluid, evolving in line with new discoveries. Despite an ever-growing record of archaeological and antiquarian surveys carried out with increasing intensity and precision, and despite warnings 'not to risk [their] neck in measuring, for the thousandth time, a Roman ruin',[51] the sites of antiquity still exerted a strong pull of attraction in the nineteenth century. Students still wanted to make their own new surveys, to explore what interested them personally.

Louis-Hippolyte Lebas (1782–1867) narrowly missed out on the French equivalent of the royal scholarship, the Prix de Rome, but he still found ways to travel extensively in Italy as a young man, partly on self-financed study tours, and partly while he was doing military service in Napoleon's newly conquered territories. A nephew of Antoine Vaudoyer, he trained in the Beaux-Arts atelier of Charles Percier, who was, in partnership with Pierre Fontaine, one of Napoleon's official architects, purveyors of the grandiose Empire or Directoire style favoured for new public monuments. Lebas, however, displayed a more rational taste in the neoclassical, and devoted much of his Italian sojourn to the study of Renaissance architecture.[52]

On tour in 1811, and working in collaboration with François Debret, who was also in Percier's studio, he prepared a comprehensive survey of Vignola's buildings, published in 1815 as *Oeuvres complètes de Jacques Barozzi de Vignole*. While mostly devoted to the major works – the Villa Farnese at Caprarola and the Villa Giulia in Rome – the final pages of the publication depict an intervention at the Palazzo Firenze in Campo Marzio in Rome. Like the Villa Giulia, the project was commissioned by the new pope, Julius III, soon after his election in 1550. But rather than being for his own use, it was for his brother's family. The work involved connecting two existing buildings through a porticoed garden to form a single residence, which was refurbished in a grand style to reflect the family's status.[53] Recent scholarship has cast doubt on Vignola's role: the architect Bartolomeo Ammannati, also employed at the Villa Giulia, appears to have been responsible for the refurbishment. What matters here, however, is that Lebas (and other eighteenth-century architects) *firmly believed* that a portion of the palazzo was the work of Vignola, based on formal similarities to the Villa Giulia.

55

*previous spread*
Soane office, view of a student on a ladder, with rod, measuring the Corinthian order, Temple of Castor and Pollux, Rome. Pencil, pen and watercolour, 940 × 634 mm © Sir John Soane's Museum, London; G L Taylor and E Cresy, Arch of Titus, from *The Architectural Antiquities of Rome*, 1821–22 © Royal Academy of Arts, London

*opposite and below*
Louis-Hippolyte Lebas, details and plan of the Palazzo Firenze, *c* 1811–15. Ink and pencil on paper, 205 × 270 mm (ceiling); 300 × 210 mm (plan)

Lebas, presumably assisted by Debret, surveyed every inch of the palazzo in a set of drawings that formed the basis for the engravings in the publication. Focusing on what he saw as Vignola's interventions – in the wing of the palazzo that marked the boundary between one trapezoid, the courtyard, and another, the garden – Lebas's survey shows us how Vignola makes the work functional in plan and dignified in elevation. The facade to the courtyard is parallel to the rest of the palazzo, unifying a central space with four pilasters marking the gateway to the garden, while the facade to the garden is rotated 30 degrees in order to make an almost square parterre landscape. Vignola makes his geometric shift – a transition hidden in the changing thickness of a tapering wall – at moments such as the threshold from courtyard to building. And he pivots a central loggia to face the garden, as its two flanking rooms attempt to mediate an equilibrium in plan by varying in competing directions. The shifting geometry of the external walls is occluded by the geometric pattern of the loggia's floor, a game of light and dark tiles rotated at 45 degrees.[54] Although Lebas measured and drew both Ammannati's

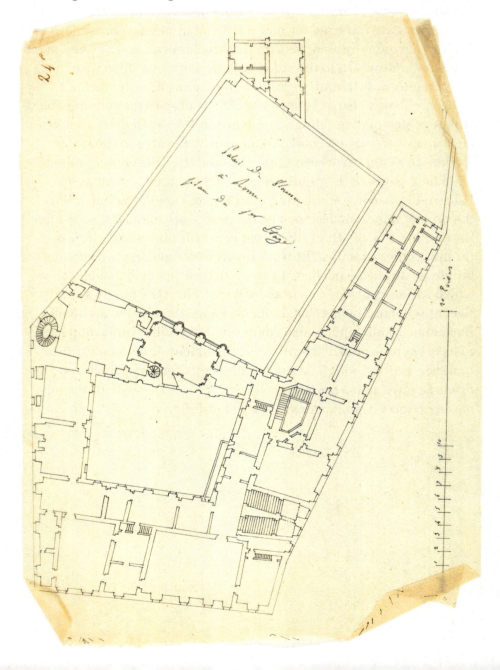

and Vignola's parts of the palazzo, it is the garden loggia that holds his attention. He surveys it with utter precision, first in plan with measurements spilling onto other sheets, then in elevation, each profile studied and quantified in lines of ink, overlaid with sections in tones of pink wash. Other elements – doorways, decoration – are treated with the same exactitude. In this way, Lebas' survey shows us how each part of Vignola's design is essential for our understanding of his work.

Detailed studies not only enhanced a student's drawing skills but also exposed them to the latest archaeological developments, allowing new discoveries to filter into contemporary architecture. In the first half of the nineteenth century there was a growing interest in the monuments along the Via Appia, and most especially in the first-century BCE Tomb of Caecilia Metella, that 'stern round tower of other days / Firm as a fortress, with its fence of stone' immortalised in Byron's *Childe Harold's Pilgrimage* (1812–18). Henri Labrouste, who won the Prix de Rome in 1824, made his own journey to the tomb at the road's three-mile marker. There, he focused on the travertine cornice of the circular monument, using grey wash to depict projection, shadow and the decorative frieze. There is a notable asymmetry to the drawing's composition. We are not quite shown a full image of the frieze, with the cropped framing suggesting a seriality to the cornice that needed to be captured in a single detailed moment. Labrouste would later adopt the mausoleum's garland as a model for the frieze of the Bibliothèque Sainte-Geneviève in Paris (1838–50), substituting a bronze roundel containing the initials of the library for the antique bucrania motif.

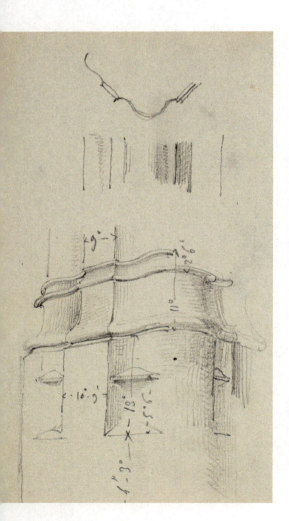

Labrouste and his fellow *pensionnaires* at the French Academy in Rome, among them Félix Duban and Léon Vaudoyer, signalled a shift in attitudes towards the survey. Whereas an older generation of academicians looked to the exemplary monuments of antiquity as the source for the idealised and abstract classical language that defined the neoclassical architecture of the French state, the younger architects focused more closely on their subjects through the lens of archaeological knowledge. Their search for a more truthful idea of the past led them to question the fundamental tenets of neoclassicism and the canonical nature of the orders. In surveys submitted as part of their residency, we see the highest possible degree of detail with a focus on the material qualities and construction of their subjects, which encompass a range of historic buildings, from Etruscan

*opposite*
Louis-Hippolyte Lebas, sketchbook detail, 1804. Pencil, 250 × 160 mm

*this page, left and below*
Henri Labrouste, tomb of Caecilia Metella (detail), 1826. Pencil and grey wash, 593 × 680 mm; C Varley, description of the camera lucida, patented by George Dollond, 1830. Beinecke Rare Book and Manuscript Library, Yale University

architecture to the Quattrocento. These drawings often examine the temporal nature of architecture by depicting individual buildings with war trophies and graffiti, or civic buildings set in an urban scene, hemmed in by blocks of everyday housing. They also considered the role played by polychromy, using new techniques such as watercolour to show the sometimes violent contrasts of colours present in the archaeological remains.

Their drawings were so accurate that the Beaux-Arts' *éminences grises* suspected them of relying too much on scientific optics, neglecting the cultivation of their artistic understanding. A letter to Léon Vaudoyer from his father Antoine sounded the alarm on the young men's use of the camera lucida. First patented in 1807, this was a small, four-sided prism on an adjustable stand.[55] If you looked through the prism what you saw was the view before you, apparently projected onto the drawing surface beneath your hand. You could then directly trace the view, avoiding the laborious process of constructing a perspective. As Barry Bergdoll has noted, new optical devices like the camera lucida reframed conceptions of the survey.[56] Rather than being seen as the surviving embodiment of classical ideals around proportion and composition, the remains of the past were objectively recorded as material artefacts – sources of architectural knowledge. From this objective certainty, aided by modern technologies of vision, a new generation could project a modern civic architecture that responded to changed economic, social and cultural conditions.

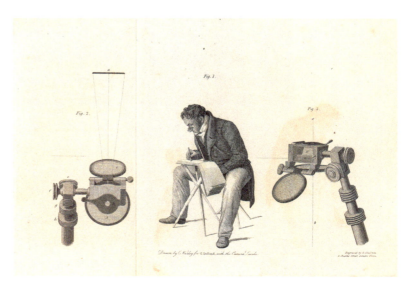

## Viollet-le-Duc: Landscapes and Restoration

Alongside new devices such as the camera lucida, new types of chemical processes began to be used to survey and mediate architecture. These techniques, in turn, changed the collective consciousness of history in Europe. The 1830s saw the invention of the first successful form of photography, the daguerreotype, which was made by exposing silver iodised plates to light. Capturing an exact reproduction of a scene, photography catered for the demand for reliable images of past architectures to support a contemporary practice threaded with Romantic historicism. And, increasingly, it supplemented more traditional means of documenting buildings: a call to expand the drawings collection of the Commission des Monuments Historiques to include daguerreotypes of important examples came from no less a personage than Baron Isidore Taylor, editor of *Voyages pittoresques et romantiques dans l'ancienne France* (1820–63), a vast compendium of lithographs surveying France's architectural history. Architects also embraced photography's potential to depict the incidental details caused by natural forces, like patina on stone or foliage on brick. While connected to broader conceptions of historical authenticity in architecture, this understanding of the photography's validity as a truthful vehicle of content was constructed outside the discipline. Total solar eclipses in 1836, 1842 and 1851 established the medium in the public eye as a means to scientifically observe natural phenomena:[57] when interpreted by an expert eye, photographs became a vital aid in authenticating claims for truth and knowledge.[58]

The French architect Eugène-Emmanuel Viollet-le-Duc (1814–1879) was initially distrustful of photography, because it seemed to reproduce the same distortions as the human eye.[59] However, we see a growing acceptance of photography as a surveying method, when its use could be systematised and controlled. In their official guidelines for the restoration of cathedrals and churches, prepared for the Ministry of Education and Religion in 1848, Viollet-le-Duc and Prosper Mérimée recommend that a series of daguerreotypes be included alongside the detailed drawings and historical sources documenting a building. Four years later, the *Encyclopédie d'architecture*, the journal of record for public works, would go one step further, ruling it inadmissible to undertake restorations without studying photographs of the existing building. In his own *Dictionnaire raisonné* (1854–68), Viollet-le-Duc describes the capacity of a photograph to offer 'an exact

 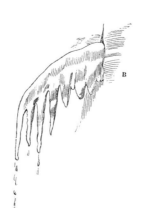 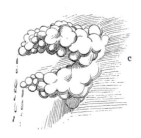

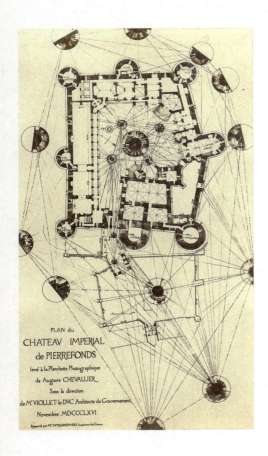

and irrefutable presentation of a building in any given state'.[60] Given this irrefutably objective quality, it is no surprise that photography was readily repurposed as a tool for generating orthographic drawings – a field of expertise we now call photogrammetry.

One of the earliest uses of photogrammetry in architecture was at the Château de Pierrefonds in Picardy, which Viollet-le-Duc restored between 1858 and 1870 at the behest of Napoleon III. In the course of the reconstruction, Viollet-le-Duc commissioned a series of 360-degree panoramic photographs of the surviving fabric,[61] which were taken with a camera ingeniously adapted to make a surveying-plane table. A series of fixed reference points for the exposures were established on and around the château. Once a sufficient number of photographs had been taken – 19 in total – lines could be traced from one to the next through parts common to both images, until the lines intersected. A third photograph was then traced across the second one, triangulating the data. Transposed onto the tracing paper, these intersections formed another reference: the translation of photographic information to a datapoint in plan. In the presentation form of this process, the 'Plan du château impérial de Pierrefonds levé à la planchette photographique de Auguste Chevallier', shown at the 1867 Exposition Universelle in Paris, we see the various stations around the château sprout overlapping and intersecting lines that are seemingly mechanically translated into a ground plan by an objective surveying process.[62] In reality, however, Chevallier's camera elongated the vertical elements of the castle, distorting their measurements – and making his invention a dead end in the mechanisation of topographic mapping.

Like Vaudoyer and Labrouste, Viollet-le-Duc spent time in Italy as a young man, though not as a *pensionnaire* at the French Academy in Rome. Always well connected – closely associated with the centres of power during the July Monarchy (1830–48), as well as the imperial court circles of Napoleon III – Viollet-le-Duc was able to choose his own path,[63] separate from the highly codified training of the Beaux-Arts. In Italy he made highly detailed drawings of monuments, depicting both their constructional qualities and their polychromatic detail. But these were not like the works of the *pensionnaires*, who as a condition of their scholarship sent both *relevés* (surveys of the existing state of a building) and *restaurations* (proposals for that building's restoration) back to Paris for assessment at various stages of their tenure.[64] Forgoing the more conventional orthographic surveys, Viollet-le-Duc relied instead on perspectival views. And unlike his friends at the academy, he made no excavations and took no measurements, nor, as he wrote in a letter to his father, did he 'draw any plans of palaces',[65] preferring instead to focus on what he called the 'general aspects' of the monuments in the spirit of contemporary painters like Jean-Auguste-Dominique Ingres or François-Marius Granet. Liberated from the strictures that had bound previous generations, Viollet-le-Duc drew pictorial surveys that offered a 'heightened record of architectural experience', with the presence of figures in historical dress and their often ritualised actions lending a narrative dimension.[66] Martin Bressani sees these images as depictions that shift time, allowing simultaneously for the restoration of the building and its historical reality. This aim extended to other sorts of scenes. In images of the ruins of antiquity – the Valley of the Temples at Agrigento, say, or the frigidarium of the Baths of Caracalla in Rome – the experience of the landscape, with the harshness of the geological forms and rough vegetation, takes precedence over the precise delineation of the buildings.

Topographic form would become an important topic for Viollet-le-Duc's later analysis, as we saw at the beginning of this book. In *Le massif du Mont Blanc* (1876), he presented a precisely measured series of drawings that documented the terrain around the highest mountain in the Alps, probing the manner and order of its geological development. Such a methodological analysis was, he noted, analogous to the architect-archaeologist's approach to studying buildings, only applied on a grander scale and relying solely on observation, in the absence of the textual sources that could be used to fill in missing elements of the built fabric.[67] Here, Viollet-le-Duc shows himself to be under the spell of the French geologist Léonce Élie de Beaumont, who argued that the world's mountain systems were linked together in a pentagonal network (*réseau*), theorising a geometrical coordination of the tectonic forces that had disturbed the earth's crust.[68] His survey of the massif attempted to quantify the effects of erosion in order to discern the landscape's underlying geometric structure. As with his work on restoring buildings, his ultimate aim was to return the mountains to an imagined original state.

Viollet-le-Duc's survey was based on empirical observation of the structure of peaks and glaciers, captured in drawings made on summer holidays over a span of eight years. Different modes of representation were used in *Le massif du Mont Blanc* to record

*previous spread*
Eugène-Emmanuel Viollet-le-Duc, *The Artist Sketching While Trapped in a Crevasse*, July 1870. Watercolour heightened with gouache, 229 × 133 mm. Katrin Bellinger Collection; Eugène-Emmanuel Viollet-le-Duc, details from *Le Massif du Mont Blanc* (below and overleaf) 1876. Bibliothèque nationale de France

*opposite*
Auguste Chevallier, photographic planchette of the Château Impérial, Pierrefonds, 1770–1871. 226 × 126 mm. Bibliothèque nationale de France

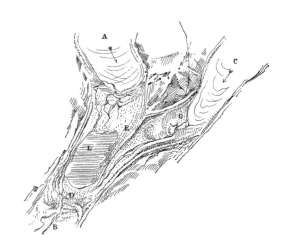

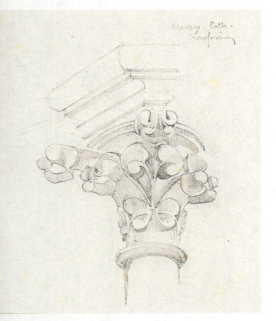

and uncover the mountain's 'origins': engraved topographical views of the Gotthard Pass, maps with arrows showing the movement associated with geological formations, and even cellular diagrams of frozen air bubbles trapped within the packed ice. The accidental played a part in the survey. Out walking with a guide on the morning of 11 July 1870, Viollet-le-Duc fell into the crevice of a glacier. Fortunately, a rope attached to his guide broke his fall. And in a further stroke of luck, he found himself face to face with something that otherwise would have gone unnoticed on his data-collecting tours: the smooth walls of azure ice that now surrounded him. While his guide went to the nearest village for help, Viollet-le-Duc made a series of drawings of the effects on the glacier of the cycle of melting and refreezing. What resulted was a different type of image, one of painterly depiction rather than objective analysis. Trapped within the glacier, he records the form of the massif across the vast sweep of geological time, viewing the violent formation of peaks and their reshaping through the processes of cooling and crystallisation. In this way, Viollet-le-Duc's analysis imposes a rational structure on the apparent chaos of the massif, drawing attention to the scientifically documented phenomena that have systematised the physical landscape.

The desire to establish an overall coherence was also a strong impulse in Viollet-le-Duc's restoration of buildings, and one that often ran counter to the desire for historical authenticity. Early works, such as his restoration of the medieval abbey church of Sainte-Madeleine at Vézelay for the newly established Commission des Monuments Historiques, show his struggle to reconcile these two strands. When he started on the work in 1840, at the tender age of 26, he was already known for his meticulous surveys of Gothic architecture. Auguste Caristie, a fellow architect and member of the commission, noted the care he took 'in reproducing exactly the form and the details that he needed to bring back to life and restore'.[69] But at Vézelay Viollet-le-Duc was confronted with complex structural problems. The church had deteriorated to such an extent that stonework crumbled in the hands of masons, and the narthex collapsed while repairs were underway, sparing only four bays in front of the transept. The commission insisted that the restoration should conform to the original, following historical examples in the choice of materials and construction techniques, and leaving no traces of the modern intervention. 'In a restoration, the first concern of the artist must be to make his work forgotten', was how Jean-Baptiste-Antoine Lassus, a pupil of Lebas and Labrouste, and Viollet-le-Duc's collaborator on Notre-Dame, described this philosophy in 1845.[70] But that 'original state' often remained hard to define in a building that had undergone centuries of modifications. Akin to archaeological fieldwork, then, the church at Vézelay was documented through an exhaustive process of description and classification. Studies were made of the beds, joints and dressings of stone. Each and every part of the building was examined through drawings, and plaster casts were made of details and textures. In March 1840 Viollet-le-Duc made a series of elevations to document the church's dilapidated condition, using a watercolour wash to indicate the crumbling stone walls. Far removed from the painterly depictions of ruins he had made on his journey to Italy, this was the survey as a precise record of a building's construction – its materials, its techniques, and ultimately its structural failures.

The analysis and repair of the structure at Vézelay would form a central part of the discussion on construction in the fourth volume of Viollet-le-Duc's *Dictionnaire raisonnée de l'architecture*, published almost 20 years later, in 1859. Here, Viollet-le-Duc illustrates how the Romanesque system of vaulting along the nave of the church evolved into an independent skeleton of ribs with webbing filling the space in between. Elsewhere in the *Dictionnaire,* detailed observations of elements such as keystones, arches and imposts are shown in sectional or exploded axonometric drawings, a form of representation recently imported from civil engineering. Unlike a perspective, the axonometric has no fixed viewpoint, no foreshortening, no background or foreground, nor absences in the drawing (dead zones). Instead, it allows for multiple components to come together (or be separated) in a single image, enabling a systematic examination of the object of study as a whole.[71]

Whether studying monuments or mountains, Viollet-le-Duc employs the same rigorous and comprehensive approach. In each of these very different settings, the survey emerges as a technique of analysing, and thereby understanding, the object of study.

Eugène-Emmanuel Viollet-le-Duc, studies of capitals (from a notebook), 1841. Pencil on paper

*Detmar Blow: The Modern Architect*

Architects on the other side of the English Channel followed Viollet-le-Duc's work with interest, often debating its merits in the clubby institutional settings that typified nineteenth-century architectural circles.[72] In 1889, fresh from a trip to France, Detmar Blow (1867–1939) gave a talk at the Architectural Association (AA) in which he described how the plan of the choir of Beauvais Cathedral relied on the geometry of the equilateral triangle, showing 'the harmonious relations between the whole and its parts'.[73] This theory was inspired by Viollet-le-Duc's geometric analysis of medieval architecture as presented in the *Dictionnaire raisonné*. One member of the audience, Arthur Beresford Pite, later known for his buildings in the Edwardian Baroque style, voiced his scepticism: personally, he was 'not fond of turning architecture into geometrical or mathematical problems'. Nevertheless, Pite did find praise for Blow's drawings, 'which had evidently been made *con amore*'. In reply, Blow said he had abandoned his original speciality – drawing orthographically using a 'hard line' technique – noting that the style, as William Burges had put it, was now only admired by 'parents, guardians, and idiots'. He had changed because John Ruskin had taught him that a more artistic method of drawing 'would not be less, but more architecturally correct' in its attempts to survey the textures and parameters of the past. These ideas were present in Ruskin's writings, typified by a passage in the *Seven Lamps of Architecture* where an engraving of the Campanile of Giotto in Florence is accompanied by the assertion that the rough, textured drawing of the tracery would 'give the reader some better conception of that tower's magnificence than the thin outlines in which it is usually portrayed'.[74]

But Ruskin's influence on Blow was not mediated purely through his writings. After winning first prize in the Class of Design at the AA the previous summer, Blow had gone on a study trip to Northern France and had met Ruskin by chance over breakfast rolls and coffee in Abbeville, where he'd stopped to sketch the cathedral.[75] This encounter would shape not only the young man's drawing style, but his whole subsequent career. Blow decided to join Ruskin, who was

*previous spread*
John Ruskin, study of Gneiss Rock, Glenfinlas, c 1853. Lampblack, body colour and pen and ink over graphite on wove paper, 478×327 mm. © University of Oxford, Ashmolean Museum

*below and following spreads*
Detmar Blow, Tintagel Old Post Office, elevations and ground plan, 1896. Pencil on paper, 180×115 mm

by then almost 70 and in poor health, on what would be his last tour of Europe, travelling through France and the Alps into Northern Italy. It was not until March 1889 that he returned to the original purpose of his trip: the survey of Beauvais Cathedral. The resulting drawings show how thoroughly he had absorbed his mentor's teachings. When they were exhibited at the AA that autumn, the *Builder* described them as being 'in Mr Ruskin's style', characterised by 'delicate handling and true rendering of effect'.[76]

'I always draw a thing exactly as it is', Ruskin noted in the *Seven Lamps of Architecture*.[77] But adherence to realism was only one part of his approach to drawing. As we see from the surveys Ruskin made during his trips to Venice, in particular during his preparation of *The Stones of Venice* (1851), the careful measurement of elements such as cornices, arch profiles and mouldings allowed him to construct typologies that could be used to chart the evolution of styles and place individual buildings within a chronological sequence. By contrast, for Blow, the survey of historic buildings was more a means of contextualisation, of storing information about places and things that might serve as points of reference, or precedents, for future work.

In addition to his study of Beauvais, like many other students at the time, Blow supplemented his education by surveying English churches and monuments, making drawings as a record of this acquired knowledge. On Saturday 17 March 1888, Blow and his AA colleague Allen Starling set out for St Nicholas at Barfreston in Kent, a twelfth-century church with Romanesque arcading. Leaving London around 7am on a chilly spring morning, they changed trains at Canterbury and then alighted at Aylesham station, from where they walked the last three miles to the church. 'We start on our way with our necessary implements', reads an annotation from the bottom of one sheet. Each man carried a board, paper, bag full of pencils and a long measuring stick. These instruments were used to make a detailed survey of the church, which they recorded in a series of sketches. It was a windy day. A drawing from Blow's sketchbook shows pencil-line gusts that first circle and then waver across the scene.

Blow later translated these sketches into a large-scale drawing of the church's west entrance and sculptural portal, as well as full-sized details of various ornaments. The drawings were exhibited at the AA's annual *conversazione*, and again at the RIBA in 1891. They were

also part of the portfolio of work that won Blow the RIBA Pugin Scholarship for measured drawings in 1892. At a meeting to announce the winners, Aston Webb singled out Blow's drawings, noting the 'most thorough and careful' depiction of the church through sketches, which 'show much appreciation of tone and colour'.[78] 'I am sure Mr Blow would tell you how much benefit he has gained by this sound and solid work', he told his audience of architects and students. That same year, Blow's pursuit of knowledge about the construction of buildings, their materials and details, would also lead him – at Ruskin's urging – to an apprenticeship with a working mason in Newcastle upon Tyne.

An interest in the skills of craftsmanship and building traditions threatened by industrialisation united a circle of young London-based architects, who included not only Blow but also William Lethaby, F W Troup and Robert Weir Schultz. Many of these architects had met in the offices of J D Sedding and Richard Norman Shaw, but from 1890 they began to gather around the Society for the Protection of Ancient Buildings (SPAB) and its Thursday evening committee meetings and press campaigns to raise awareness of conservation

issues. As in their student days, many of them also devoted their Saturdays to surveying endangered buildings.

Blow became involved with the SPAB in the repair of a small medieval house, known as the Old Post Office, in Tintagel. By the late nineteenth century, visitors were flocking to the North Cornwall coast in large numbers, drawn by the romance of Arthurian legends popularised by Tennyson and, ironically, that leading light of the SPAB and the Arts and Crafts movement, William Morris. Historic buildings were being pulled down to make way for new shops, hotels and boarding houses. When the Old Post Office was put up for auction in September 1895 a local painter, Constance Phillott, alerted the SPAB to the risk it would be demolished if purchased by an ambitious hotelier.[79] A sympathetic local resident, Catherine Johns, stepped in and bought the building, while Phillott's artist friends in Cornwall and London donated paintings to raise funds for the necessary repairs.[80] The SPAB committee was willing to help Phillott administer the work on condition that it was 'carried out in accordance with the views of the society'.[81] In other words, *repair* rather than attempt to restore a stylistic unity, in the manner of Viollet-le-Duc. This

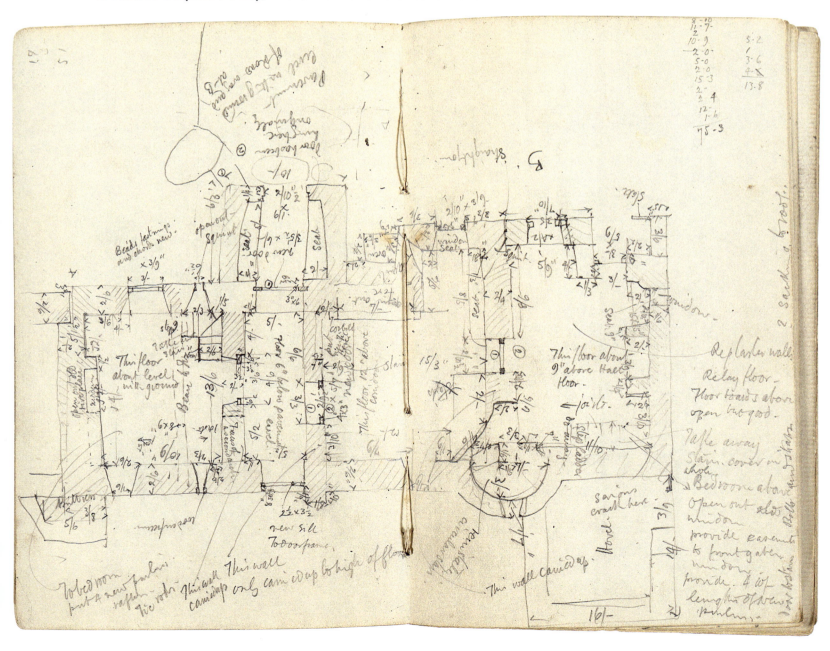

Detmar Blow, 'A Wren House at Chichester', 1896. Pencil on paper, 180 × 115 mm

approach followed William Morris's admonition to 'to resist all tampering with either the fabric or ornament of the building as it stands'.[82] The SPAB's secretary, Thackeray Turner, also had a quibble regarding Blow's terms for accepting the commission: 'everything seems perfectly satisfactory with the exception of the question of the expense in making a survey', and particular the 'heavy railway fare'.[83] By the 1890s improvements in the railway infrastructure had radically changed the possibilities for architectural practice. Architects based in London could now travel around the country, personally supervising the surveying or construction of half a dozen buildings at once – something that would have been inconceivable to their eighteenth-century predecessors.[84] Thanks to advances in communications technologies, they could also intervene remotely – not always to good effect. J D Sedding had criticised the type of architect who worked as a 'distant dictator who uses the agency of post and telegram to communicate his wishes'. He believed the 'real architect of a building ... must be his own clerk of works, his own carver, his own director; he must be the familiar spirit of the structure as it rises from the ground'.[85] Early in his career, Blow was all of those things. Embracing

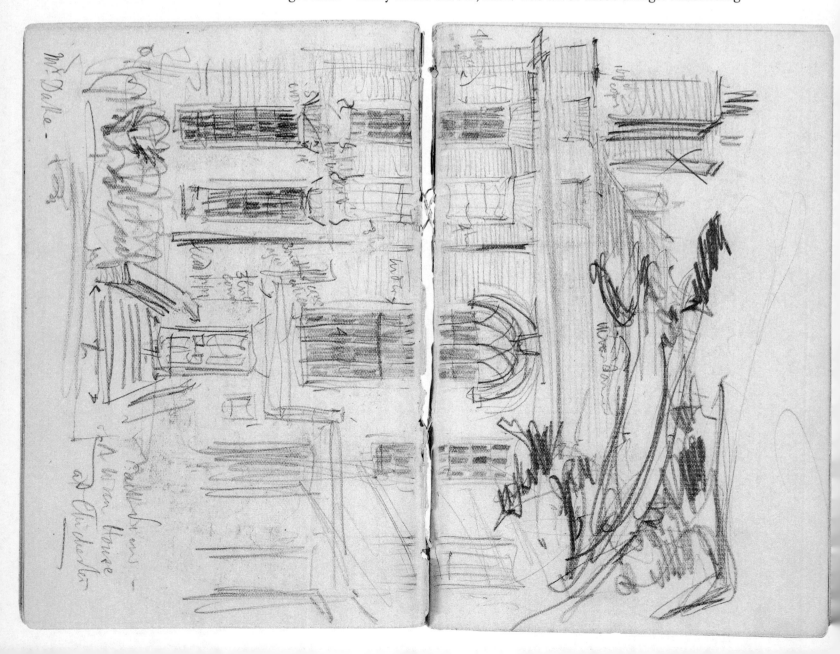

the role of the 'wandering architect', he travelled, like an artisan, with his own band of masons. A brother of the Art Workers' Guild from 1892, his survey work was based on a fundamental understanding of craft-based building techniques, honed by the studies he had made on his travels as a student.[86]

A sketchbook survey of the Old Post Office from early 1896 shows us this approach. The plan, covered in extensive annotations, records in detail the dimensions, condition and materials of the surviving fabric. As Blow's pupil Herbert North described the experience a few months later: 'We have been unearthing all kinds of interesting squints, corbels and things that remind people of the beautiful simplicity of the life of their ancestors.'[87] This past would resurface in the present, as the survey made its mark on other projects Blow was working on at the time. The late-medieval newel staircase at Tintagel, with its external expression on the facade, appears first in Blow's work on two Arts and Crafts 'cottages': Long Copse in Surrey, a collaboration with Alfred H Powell, and Stoneywell Cottage in Leicestershire, built with and for the furniture designer and architect Ernest Gimson.

Much of the picturesque quality of the Old Post Office derived from the accretions of time. In the sketchbook, three pages of elevations show us the building's outline, with a hint of perspective to allude to its three-dimensional form. Quickly shaded pencil marks depict irregular stones and tiles and vegetation. The careful attention devoted to these features in the drawing was carried into the restoration work. A letter from Constance Phillott to the SPAB praised Blow for removing the 'modern rubbish', restoring the central hall and newel staircase, and ensuring that the cottage's 'picturesque character ... and the ferns and mosses on the roof, and the ivy on its walls ... [was] quite un-hurt by the workmen'.[88] The preservation of this patina clearly relates not only to the SPAB's attitude to heritage but also to the belief of Blow's mentor, Ruskin, that the 'truth' of architecture was to be obtained through this type of practised observation, recorded through drawing. Knowledge of the natural world and the built environment could be filtered through the perception of the individual. It does not 'matter much what things are in themselves, but only what they are to us', was how Ruskin had put it in the *Modern Painters*.[89] Here, one individual, Detmar Blow, adopts the survey to comprehend the textures of the past and the details and the construction of historic buildings. His surveys record the symbols of a lost way of life that can be restored for the present day.

73

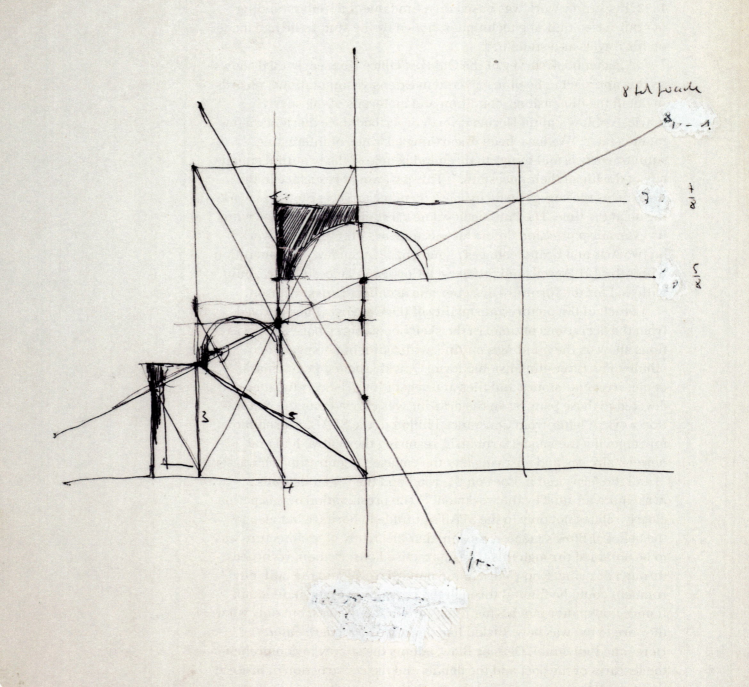

S. Lorenzo
Florenz

*Peter Märkli: The Search for Certainty*

Reinterpreting the past, tuning it to the demands of modern life, is an impulse that also runs through more recent surveys made in the past 30 years. Throughout his career the Swiss architect Peter Märkli (1953–) has made analytical drawings of historic buildings. Surveying the past from his desk, he searches for underlying principles of composition using a framework of ruled lines that represent the contours of buildings, structuring the outlines of their interiors and materials. For instance, a drawing of San Lorenzo in Florence – not exactly the simplest object to represent – dispenses with our memories of the building, say the grand dome or the unfinished front facade. Instead, focusing on the sectional volumes of nave, aisle and chapel, Märkli reduces the building to its formal essence. The coffered ceiling is absent, as is the articulated structure in *pietra serena* and all of the interior decoration. In their place, a diagrammatic section delineates the interior with absolute economy. A vertical centre line holds the middle of the drawing, setting up the proportional relationship between the related parts of the geometric system: a horizontal line (the soffit), a vertical line (the line of columns), and the arch of the crossing where the nave meets the transept. Adjacent to this central portion, Märkli records the horizontal module of 2:1 between nave and aisle, while the vertical system takes in a series of interlocked proportions that hold together the capitals of the columns, the springing of the arches, and the chapels on the basilica's perimeter.

Remaking buildings on his own terms through the survey was where architecture began for Märkli. As a student at ETH Zurich in the 1970s, he sat in lectures where Bernhard Hoesli would present with absolute certainty the canonical works of modern architecture – more often than not buildings by Le Corbusier.[90] Märkli was not so sure that these highly refined buildings reflected the fundamental questions of architecture, so he attempted to answer these questions for himself by making drawings: 'I had to start with the simplest things that I could look at and comprehend'.[91] Drawing became a means to return to the first principles and in particular to the question of why the proportions of particular buildings have a resonance across time. In his first semester at university, on being asked to create a sketch and then turn it into a plan, he developed his own proportional system, in the process gaining a means of expression, or language, of his own. For Märkli, it is in part the necessary precision of proportional

75

*previous spread*
Peter Märkli, Basilica di San Lorenzo, Florence, section, *c* 1988. Ballpoint pen on trace, with white Tippex, 314×235 mm

*opposite*
Peter Märkli, Hagia Sophia, Istanbul, elevation, *c* 1988. Ballpoint pen on trace, with white Tippex, 270×310 mm

systems that separates architecture from the other visual arts: 'We can't just proceed empirically or emotionally like in painting or sculpture; instead, we have to have absolute certainty in terms of the proportions.'[92]

This search for certainty would uncover a range of different references for Märkli: the Golden Section, the Middle Eastern dome construction with the 5:4:3 triangle; then the proportional systems of artists such as Leonardo da Vinci, Dürer and Rembrandt. His drawings of these systems explore ways to divide the human figure in eight parts, within the intersection of a circle and a square. Diagonal lines cut across the geometric figures of body, circle, square, showing the proportional relationships between navel, shoulders, feet. In Märkli's words, these 'proportions are a tool' for the architect: they set limits on the work that are defined, not by a minimalist agenda, but by a desire for clarity and exactitude.[93] We see this in another drawing, a desktop study of Hagia Sophia. The fundamental and memorable image of the building is captured in the section: a nave covered by a vast dome, flanked on either side by aisles with half-domes, and arcades of arched windows. Overlaid onto this base is the outline of a circle and then a series of lines that pick out the exact proportional relationships (7/8 and 5/8) between the parts – wall, cornice, dome – and the whole. These drawings are surveys in the sense that they analyse an object and form a reference. They show clear evidence of a systematic study, where a building is excavated and its underlying proportional principles are unearthed.[94] Märkli describes Piet Mondrian's paintings in a similar fashion, noting 'Had they not the proportions that they have, they would have no tension, nothing.'[95]

In the first part of this text, we considered how architects use the survey as a reference to establish certainty in their work. Märkli's studies attempt to avoid the doubt that besets most architects, though they rarely admit it out loud. In a sense, these drawings represent a search for order and precision in the low-rise, solitary, suburban sites of Märkli's early work. In those private houses, small apartment buildings and artists' studios, Märkli turns the focus from the certainty of canonical buildings to the new values of contemporary society. And as architects have done over the centuries, Märkli looks to quarry the past for the production of new architecture.

Certainty is at the heart of the survey. It informs how we see the world and how we construct it. As architects, it is where we start a project and begin our education, whether we are recording the known world on site or surveying the canon from our desk. The survey is a reference; it is a form of knowledge, framing both information and content alike. In each of these guises the survey offers control by establishing principles that give order to the built environment, allowing us to comprehend it. We have also seen how the survey is a projective technique, recording what has gone before in terms of the present, and in a tone modulated by the individual surveyor and their objectives. Not purely an architectural artefact, the survey is also political, ideological and temporal. It is intertwined with the practice of individual architects and with collective identities, implicated in their work and ours, in the past, present and future. There is no architecture without the survey.

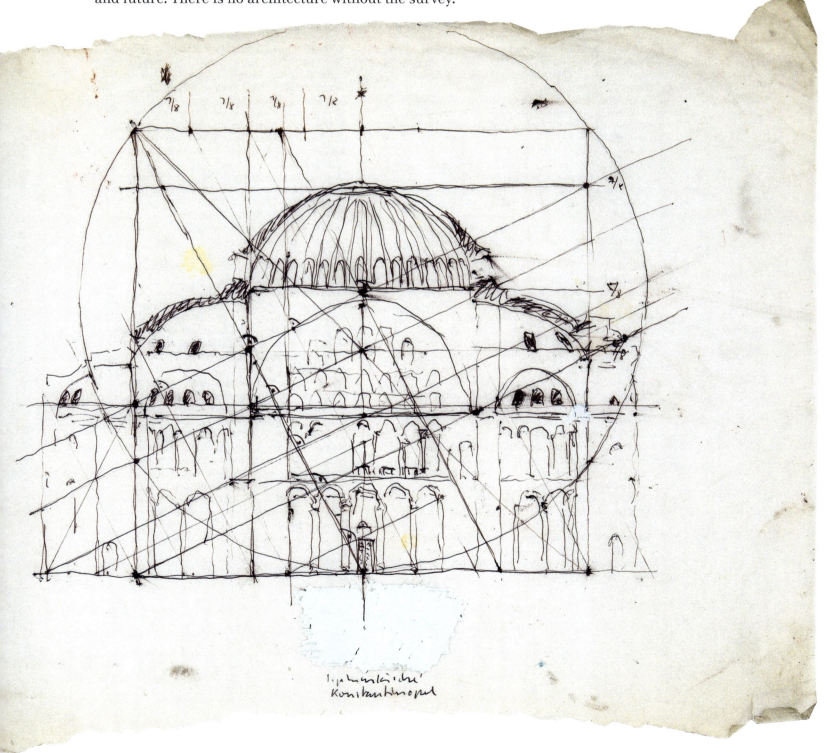

1. The project is instigated and led by the Chair for the Theory of Architecture Prof Dr Laurent Stalder, with Tobias Erb and Mélissa Vrolixs.
2. 'Eduardo Souto de Moura, Álvaro Siza', in Kate Goodwin, ed, *Sensing Spaces, Architecture Reimagined* (London, 2014), 183.
3. Complementary to both purposes was the survey's role as a form of scholarly evidence, which allowed architects to demonstrate their understanding of Roman models to potential patrons.
4. As we know from the frequently cited passage in the letter Raphael wrote to Pope Leo X. See John Shearman, *Raphael in Early Modern Sources: 1483–1602* (New Haven and London, 2003), vol 1, 527–45. The objectivity of orthographic drawing has of course been questioned by others who reject the single-author narrative of orthography and its socio-political power as a representational technique.
5. Rudolf Wittkower, *Architectural Principles in the Age of Humanism*, third edition reprint (London, 1971), 75.
6. 'Architect', *The Builders' Dictionary or Architect's Companion* (London, 1734).
7. C F Roland le Virloys, *Dictionnaire d'architecture* (Paris, 1770), 186.
8. See E Schroeder Prior, *Cathedral Builders in England* (London, 1905).
9. J C Loudon, 'The Estimate and Costs of a Building', *Architectural Magazine* (September 1835), 404.
10. 'Survey', *Architectural Dictionary* (London, 1893), vol 6, 127.
11. This happened to me.
12. E Panofsky, *Perspective as Symbolic Form*, trans Christopher S Wood (New York, 1997), 67.
13. 'Alberto Ponis in Conversation with Jonathan Sergison', *AA Files* 73 (2016), 112.
14. Ibid, 113.
15. Ibid, 112.
16. Kevin Lynch, *Site Planning*, third edition (Cambridge MA, 1984), 385.
17. Ibid, 386.
18. Nicholas Olsberg, 'The Very Grammar of the Art', in Desley Luscombe, Helen Thomas and Niall Hobhouse, eds, *Architecture through Drawing* (London, 2019), 102.
19. See, among others, Nilanjana Mukherjee, '"A Desideratum More Sublime": Imperialism's Expansive Vision and Lambton's Trigonometrical Survey of India', *Postcolonial Studies* 14:4 (2011), 429–47; Brenna Bhandar, *Colonial Lives of Property: Law, Land, and Racial Regimes of Ownership, Global and Insurgent Legalities* (Durham, 2018), 6; James C Scott, *Seeing like a State: How Certain Schemes to Improve the Human Condition Have Failed* (New Haven, 2008), 47–52.
20. *Proceedings of the Institute of British Architects: Sessions 1842–1849*, 213–14. The model was exhibited by T L Donaldson, considered the 'father of the profession' in Britain and a professor at University College, London.
21. 'Forensic Medicine', *Edinburgh Medical and Surgical Journal*, May 1847, 865.
22. 'Influence of Early Buildings on the Architecture of all Countries – The Chinese Model of a House now in this Country', *Builder*, 6 March 1847, 105.
23. Ibid.
24. Sibel Acar, 'Intersecting Routes of Architectural Travel, Photography, and Survey Books in the Nineteenth Century', in Micheline Nilsen, ed, *Nineteenth-Century Photographs and Architecture: Documenting History, Charting Progress, and Exploring the World* (London, 2013), 79–80.
25. James Fergusson, *Picturesque Illustrations of Ancient Architecture in Hindostan* (London, 1847).
26. Itohan Osayimwese, 'Prolegomenon to an Alternative Genealogy of German Modernism: German Architects' Encounters with World Cultures c 1900', *Journal of Architecture* 18:6 (2013), 845.
27. Itohan Osayimwese, *Colonialism and Modern Architecture in Germany: Culture, Politics and the Built Environment* (Pittsburgh, 2017).
28. My thanks to Neil Bingham for his help on this aspect of the education at the Royal Academy.
29. Although the design was Soane's, it is likely Dance assisted him with the initial *parti*. See Jill Lever, 'The Soane–Dance collaboration, 1771–1799', *Architectural History* 53 (2010), 165.
30. Pierre de la Ruffinière du Prey, 'Soane and Hardwick in Rome: A Neo-Classical Partnership', *Architectural History* 15 (1972), 51, quotes: SM, Correspondence Cupboard 2, division xiv, B(1), item lb, 1 August 1778, letter from John Soane to Henry Wood.
31. John Soane, 'Lecture III', in David Watkin, ed, *Sir John Soane: Enlightenment Thought and the Royal Academy Lectures* (Cambridge/New York, 1996), 525. Soane chose to illustrate this point not with the section, but with a plan presumably redrawn by an assistant.
32. Henry Lemonnier, *Procès-verbaux de l'Académie Royale d'Architecture*, vol 8, 1768–1779 (Paris, 1911), 341–42.
33. Quoted in Reinhard Wegner and Margarete Kühn, eds, *Die Reise nach Frankreich und England im Jahre 1826* (Munich, 1990), 117.
34. Ibid, 136–37.
35. Soane, 'Lecture XII', in Watkin, *Sir John Soane*, 657.
36. Ibid.
37. In this opinion I defer to the numerous editions of William St Clair, *Lord Elgin and the Marbles* (London, 1967).
38. Luigi Beschi suggests a date of 1813 for the survey. See 'CH R Cockerell e il Partenone', *Annuario della Scuola archeologica di Atene e delle missioni italiane in Oriente*, 87 (2009), 121.
39. Frank Salmon, 'C R Cockerell and the Discovery of Entasis in the Columns of the Parthenon', in F Salmon, ed, *The Persistence of the Classical: Essays on Architecture Presented to David Watkin* (London, 2008), 106–23.
40. My thanks to Frank Salmon for his help on this point. For the long history on the accuracy of the measurements made by British architects in Athens see F Salmon, 'The Ideal and the Real in British Hellenomania, 1751–1851', in K Harloe, N Momigliano and A Farnoux, eds, *Hellenomania* (London, 2018), 73–99.

41  See Charles Robert Cockerell, *Travels in Southern Europe and the Levant 1810–1817. The Journal of C R Cockerell, RA.* (London, 1903), 44–45 Cockerell's travelogue was edited by his son, Samuel Pepys Cockerell.

42  Peter Oluf Brøndsted, *Reisen und Untersuchungen in Griechenland*, vol 2 (Paris, 1830), 293. The frontispiece of the volume was dedicated to Cockerell and Bertel Thorvaldsen for their studies on the Parthenon.

43  Ibid.

44  Cockerell, *Travels in Southern Europe and the Levant*, 6–14. On its return to England the *Black Joke* was captured by French privateers off Algeria and its cargo stolen, including all of the letters and drawings Cockerell had made on his outbound voyage.

45  Ibid, 43.

46  Ibid, 53.

47  Susan Pearce, *Charles Robert Cockerell in the Mediterranean* (Woodbridge, Suffolk, 2017), 140, quotes a letter from C R Cockerell to John Cockerell, 13 May 1811.

48  Cockerell, *Travels in Southern Europe and the Levant*, 51.

49  The 'authentic record' of these 'investigations', as Cockerell called them in the foreword, was published some 50 years later. Charles Robert Cockerell, *The Temples of Jupiter Panhellenius at Aegina and of Apollo Epicurius at Bassae near Phigaleia in Arcadia* (London, 1860).

50  Cockerell, *Travels in Southern Europe and the Levant*, 57.

51  Frank Salmon, *Building on Ruins: The Rediscovery of Rome and English Architecture* (Aldershot, 2000), 65, quotes George Wightwick, 'Sketches by a Travelling Architect', *Library of the Fine Arts* (London, 1831), 29.

52  Lebas came second in the Grand Prix of 1804. He is best known for his career as an official architect in the early nineteenth century and his teaching at the École des Beaux-Arts, where he was professor of architectural history from 1840 until 1863, when he was displaced by Viollet-le-Duc.

53  For the complex history of the project see Maria Giulia Aurigemma, *Palazzo Firenze in Campo Marzio* (Rome, 2007).

54  Manuel Montenegro once pointed out something similar to me at FAUP by Álvaro Siza in Porto. In a space with two non-perpendicular walls, Siza rotates the grid of the marble floor 45 degrees so that the eye fails to notice the irregular geometry of the inflected walls.

55  Gaby Wood's recent essay on using a camera lucida in 2020 is highly enjoyable: Gaby Wood, 'Diary: How to draw an albatross', *London Review of Books* 42:12 (18 June 2020), 36–37.

56  Barry Bergdoll, 'A Matter of Time: Architects and Photographers in Second Empire France', in Malcolm Daniel, *The Photographs of Édouard Baldus* (New York, 1994), 101.

57  Jan Golinski, *Making Natural Knowledge: Constructivism and the History of Science*, second edition (Cambridge/New York, 2005), 159.

58  As the nineteenth century progressed, the transition from direct experience (pupillage system, Grand Tour) to formalised knowledge (university education, building regulations, professional organisations) was central to the construction of the architect's position and authority in society. The survey – adapted through its codification in handbooks and the adoption of new technologies like photography – would remain a key part of this construction.

59  For a discussion on this distrust see Lauren M O'Connell, 'Viollet-le-Duc on drawing, photography, and the "space outside the frame"', *History of Photography* 22:2 (1988), 139–46.

60  Eugène-Emmanuel Viollet-le-Duc, *The Foundations of Architecture: Selections from the Dictionnaire raisonné*, trans Kenneth Whitehead (New York, 1990), 225.

61  I rely here on Aron Vinegar's excellent essay 'Panoramic Photography as Imagination Technology: Viollet-le-Duc and the Restoration of the Château de Pierrefonds', in Z Arnold et al, eds, *Eugène-Emmanuel Viollet-le-Duc: Internationales Kolloquium* (Zurich, 2010), 90–111.

62  As the user rotated to expose the plate around 360 degrees, the *planchette photographique* allowed a portion of the preceding image sequence to follow onto the next one. Rather than a continuous image, it produced a sequence of overlapping images, which made for both confusion and inaccuracy during the retroactive process of topographical mapping.

63  See Martin Bressani, *Architecture and the Historical Imagination: Eugène-Emmanuel Viollet-le-Duc, 1814–1879* (Oxford/New York, 2017), 99, for a discussion of Viollet-le-Duc's social standing.

64  These drawings were also known as *état actuel* (a survey of the existing fabric) and *état restauré* (an idealised reconstruction of a building). The former type was accompanied by a written description of the age, condition and construction of the monument.

65  Letter of 29 August 1836, quoted in Bressani, *Architecture and the Historical Imagination*, 67, footnote 6.

66  Bressani, *Architecture and the Historical Imagination*, 71.

67  Ibid, 481, footnote 63.

68  Jacques Touret. 'Élie de Beaumont (1798–1874), des systèmes de montagnes au réseau pentagonal', *Travaux du Comité français d'Histoire de la Géologie*, third series, 21 (2007), 127–55.

69  Kevin Murphy, *Memory and Modernity: Viollet-le-Duc at Vézelay* (University Park, Penn., 2000), 92.

70  Quoted in Bressani, *Architecture and the Historical Imagination*, 107.

71  Yve-Alain Bois, 'Metamorphosen der Axonometrie', *Daidalos* 1 (1981) 40–58; Thierry Mandoul, 'From Rationality to Utopia: Auguste Choisy and Axonometric Projection', in Mario Carpo and Frédérique Lemerle, eds, *Perspective Projections & Design: Technologies of Architectural Representation* (London, 2008), 151–62; Carlotta Darò, 'Sound Conduits: Displaying the Architecture of Telecommunications', in *Architecture/Machine: Programs, Processes, and Performances*, gta Papers 1 (2017), 110–23.

72 Viollet-le-Duc corresponded frequently with the Royal Institute of British Architects, who awarded him their Royal Gold Medal in 1864.

73 This and subsequent quotes from the lecture are from 'A Travelling Student's Notes: A Paper by Mr D J Blow, Travelling Student of the Architectural Association', *Builder*, 28 May 1889, 394–96.

74 John Ruskin, *The Works of John Ruskin, Volume 8: The Seven Lamps of Architecture*, Edward Tyas Cook and Alexander Wedderburn, eds (London, 1903), 187–88.

75 'Croydon School of Art', *Croydon Advertiser and East Surrey Reporter* (24 January 1885); 'Royal Academy: Architecture School', *Builder*, 14 July 1888, 30; 'The Opening Conversazione of the Architectural Association', *Builder*, 13 October 1888, 270.

76 'The Architectural Association Conversazione', *Builder*, 12 October 1889, 256.

77 Ruskin, *The Seven Lamps of Architecture*, 186.

78 'A Review of the Students' Work', *Builder*, 30 January 1892, 81.

79 SPAB Archive, The Old Post Office, Tintagel, letter from Thackeray Turner to Detmar Blow, 31 January 1896.

80 SPAB Archive, letter from Thackeray Turner to Detmar Blow, 16 March 1896.

81 SPAB Archive, letter from Detmar Blow to Thackeray Turner, 6 February 1896. Two days later Blow replied to say that he would be pleased to go down to Tintagel after 15 February.

82 William Morris, 'Restoration', *Athenaeum*, 2591 (23 June 1877), 807.

83 SPAB Archive, letter from Detmar Blow to Thackeray Turner, 6 February 1896.

84 Howard Colvin, *Biographical Dictionary of English Architects* (London, 1954), 24.

85 John Dando Sedding, 'Architecture: Old and New', *British Architect* 15 (1881), 229.

86 After the survey, however, Blow delegated his role on site to Herbert North, one of his pupils, and Henry Wilson, who was then running what remained of J D Sedding's office. Blow's absence from the restoration work in Cornwall is possibly explained by the demands of another project he was working on at the time, Long Copse in Surrey.

87 SPAB Archive, letter from Herbert North to Thackeray Turner, May 1896.

88 SPAB Archive, letter from Constance Phillott to Thackeray Turner, 23 November 1896.

89 John Ruskin, *Modern Painters*, vol 5 (London, 1860), 202.

90 Hoesli had worked for Le Corbusier before moving to the US to teach at the University of Texas School of Architecture between 1951 and 1958, alongside Colin Rowe, John Hejduk, Robert Slutzky, Werner Seligmann and others, a group later known as the Texas Rangers.

91 'Peter Märkli in conversation with Elena Markus', in Pamela Johnston, ed, *Everything one invents is true* (Lucerne, 2017), 19.

92 'Peter Märkli: History, Typology, Invention', in Marc Angélil and Jörg Himmelreich, eds, *Architecture Dialogues: Positions – Concepts – Visions* (Zurich, 2011), 268.

93 Peter Märkli, 'Indestructible Solidity', in Andri Gerber, Tibor Joanelly and Oya Atalay Franck, eds, *Proportions and Cognition in Architecture and Urban Design* (Berlin, 2019), 125.

94 Ibid, 121. When a new employee begins at Märkli's, the first thing they have to learn is how the proportional systems of measurement develop in the office's work. Märkli stipulates the first measurement, the fundamental framework for the design, derived from the study of the building's programme. This is followed by other spacing measurements, which can only be divided by even numbers on account of the overall proportional system. These initial references can originate in a variety of sources: the building's cross section (Synthes headquarters), ceiling heights (Im Birch school), or the organisational module of an office (Novartis). These proportional relationships provide a particular relationship between design and construction. Later, on the construction site, Märkli and his colleagues may adjust the resonance of an interior wall or a window within the building's overall composition by moving the two lines of a wall back and forth across the floorplan, in increments or eighths or sixteenths. Märkli has argued that a builder will not interfere because such small adjustments are not relevant to their cost calculations and scheduling.

95 Martin Steinmann, 'You See What You See – Reflections on a New Work by Peter Märkli', *a+u* 329 (February 1998), 5.

1. Città — E. F. d.
2. Boschetto, e Giardini reali — E. d.
3. Campo di Marte — E. e.

*Plates*

Better known in his lifetime as a painter, Charles Stanislas L'Éveillé trained as an engineer at the École des Ponts et Chaussées and then worked as assistant to René Girard, the chief engineer of the Ourcq Canal, a major Napoleonic infrastructure project that bends out of Paris to the northwest. As an artist, L'Éveillé almost always worked in albums and sketchbooks, observing landscapes, buildings and people during his travels around France, Italy, Greece and Turkey. In this watercolour, he surveys both the medieval ruins and, in the lower right a group of young students who are themselves drawing the ruins. On the one hand we can see this caprice as a genre painting of a fallen Gothic building, overtaken by the forces of time and nature. On the other hand, L'Éveillé's education might suggest an individual interest in the performance of structure or the monumentality and temporality of materials ahead of a Romantic depiction of contemporary life.

*pl. 1*   Charles Stanislas L'Éveillé, capriccio of a Gothic ruin, *c* 1805. Black ink, watercolour and gouache on laid paper, 307 × 385 mm

The subjective vagaries of perception can affect the nature of the survey, its method and its content. Le Corbusier saw the view from the air as a new sensory experience. This gave rise to a new standard of measurement fundamental for the production of modern architecture.

When Le Corbusier visited South America in 1929, travelling by ship from France to Buenos Aires, he met a group of young French aviators who were developing air mail delivery routes across the continent – a network designed to compensate for the poor communications infrastructure in its hinterland, neglected by the extractive colonial economic system. Jean Mermoz and Antoine de Saint-Exupéry flew him across the expansive coastal plains of Brazil and Uruguay. He surveyed the continent from above, a viewpoint that brought out the strong contrast between the wide tropical landscape and what he saw as the sprawling urban centres.

Crucially, this aerial journey was a projective survey rather than a record. From the plane, above Rio de Janeiro, Le Corbusier drew an elevated highway, a new type of infrastructure that would connect apartment blocks on a colossal scale, set above the existing buildings. From this privileged position in the sky, Le Corbusier noted that everything became clear.

*pl. 2*  Le Corbusier, *Urbanisme*, Rio de Janeiro, Brazil, 1929. © FLC/ADAGP

Three days after her arrival in Brazil, the Italian architect Lino Bo Bardi made this drawing of a public park in Rio de Janeiro, her first record of the city. In the background, we have lush trees and billboards surrounding the crowds as they move through the traffic and the rain. At centre, two men sit on top of a grocery truck as if they were on a carnival float. What Bo Bardi records is the image of a large, cosmopolitan city, one that is both exuberant and full of contrasts. Her drawing shows us the different worlds that coexist in Brazilian society: the formality and the wealth, alongside the spontaneity and the poverty. These two worlds would go on to nurture her identification with Brazil and populate her imagination.

*pl. 3*  Lina Bo Bardi, Passeio Público park and theatre district, Rio de Janeiro, 1946.
Watercolour and India ink on paper 242 × 223 mm, ILBPMB Archives

For a Renaissance architect the study of the antique was the study of the basic principles of design. Sixteenth-century drawings of antiquities cannot be judged by a single set of standards because each artist had their own particular aims in depicting the architecture of the past.

This sheet is a part of a larger corpus of drawings of antique subjects, generally attributed to the Workshop of Antonio da Sangallo the Younger, although the art historian Arnold Nesselrath has recently indicated that they are more likely to be the work of Giovanni Antonio Dosio. Here the draughtsman is interested in using orthographic elevation to record in the most objective manner the proportions and dimensions of various columns, their bases and entablatures. The elements are carefully measured but mostly drawn in quick, loose linework, with the author moving from one subject to another at speed.

*pl. 4*  Giovanni Antonio Dosio, plans and details from an album, after 1550. Ink on oiled paper, 215 × 300 mm

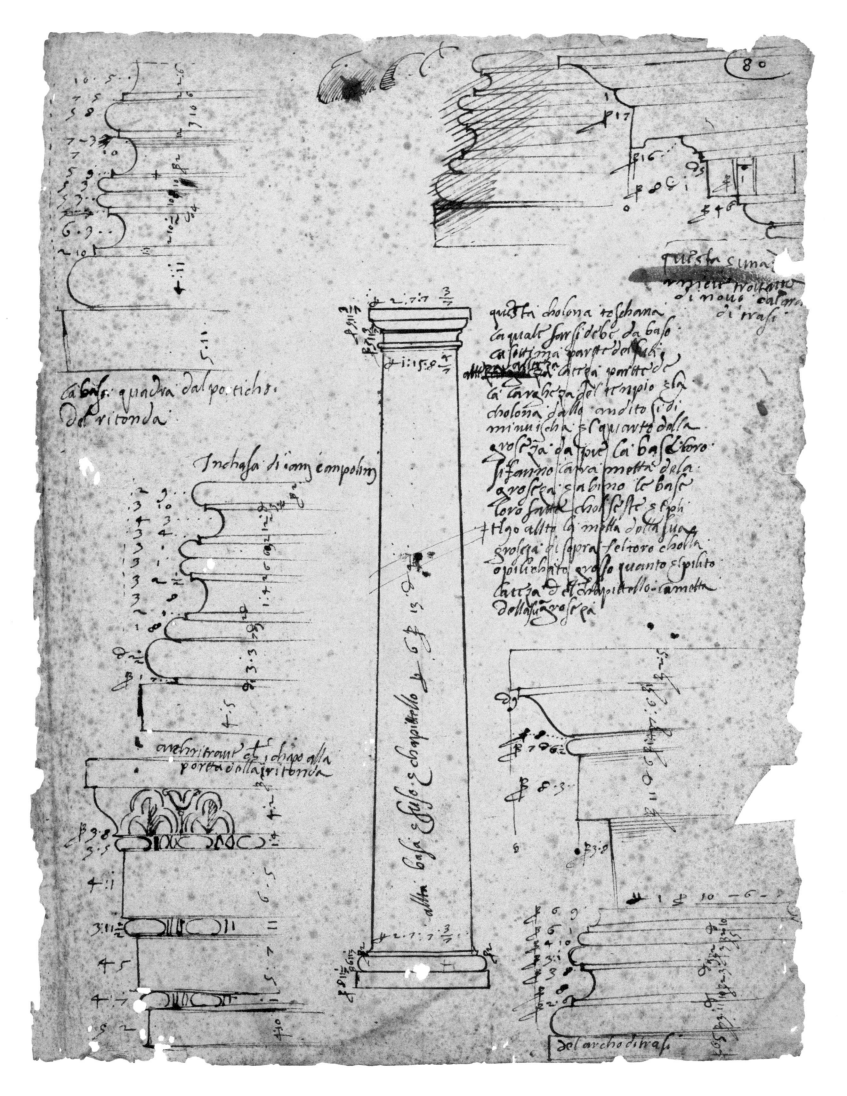

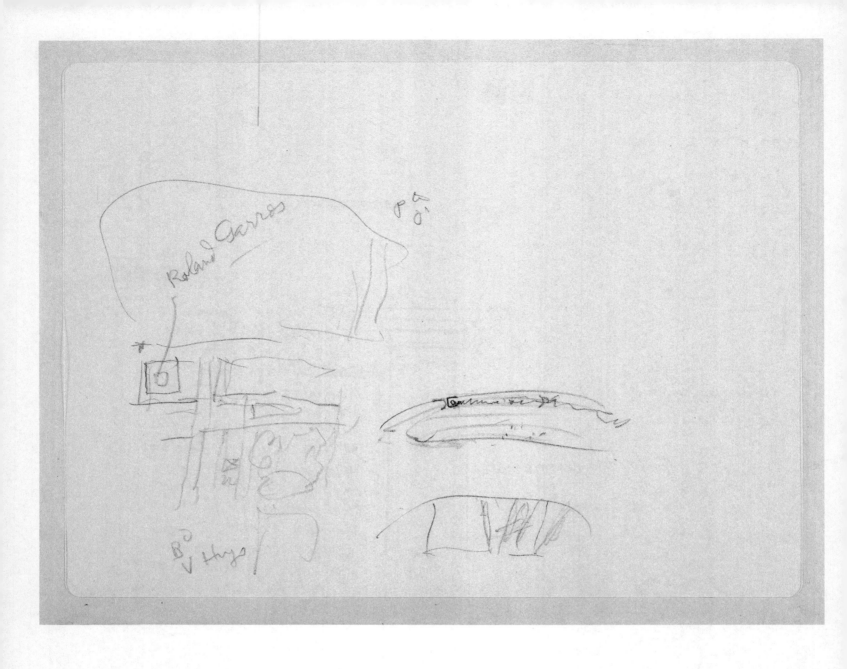

In July 1958, one day before Faisal II was assassinated during the 14 July Revolution in Baghdad, the Iraqi Ministry of Development sent a telegram to Paris confirming Le Corbusier's appointment to design the Olympic Stadium. Over the following months, while the programme and site were being clarified, his office conducted a broad study of international precedents for the design and construction of the modern stadium complex, ranging from stadiums in Berlin and Bogotá, to gymnasiums in Stockholm and Tokyo and, closer to home, two major sites near Le Corbusier's Paris apartment: the Parc de Prince stadium and Roland Garros tennis complex. Two sketch surveys of the Stade Roland Garros record in rough pencil the constellation of buildings on a polygonal site, held between two roads. The more northerly road, Avenue de la Porte d'Auteuil, separated the tennis complex from the Bois de Boulogne, the remnants of an ancient oak forest turned public park. To the east, Le Corbusier marks the vague outline of the Jardin des Serres d'Auteuil, a botanical garden with

greenhouses filled with the sorts of tropical plants that would be used in the landscaping of the Baghdad project. To the southeast was the Piscine Molitor, a courtyard block on a triangular site that included a T-shaped outdoor swimming pool. The relationship between this loose survey of his own neighbourhood and the proposals for Baghdad are clear. Le Corbusier is trying to understand how a complex can be held together, despite the disparate parts and programmes split into different buildings and dissected by roads. His drawing takes command of the site, abstracting the relevant buildings, and only focuses on the elements he needs, neglecting neighbouring infill city blocks or housing. The change in Iraq's leadership does not seem to have affected the design: the royal box was renamed the presidential box.

*pl. 5–6*  Le Corbusier, Roland Garros and Parc de Prince stadiums, Paris, 1958. Pencil on calque, 273 × 210 mm

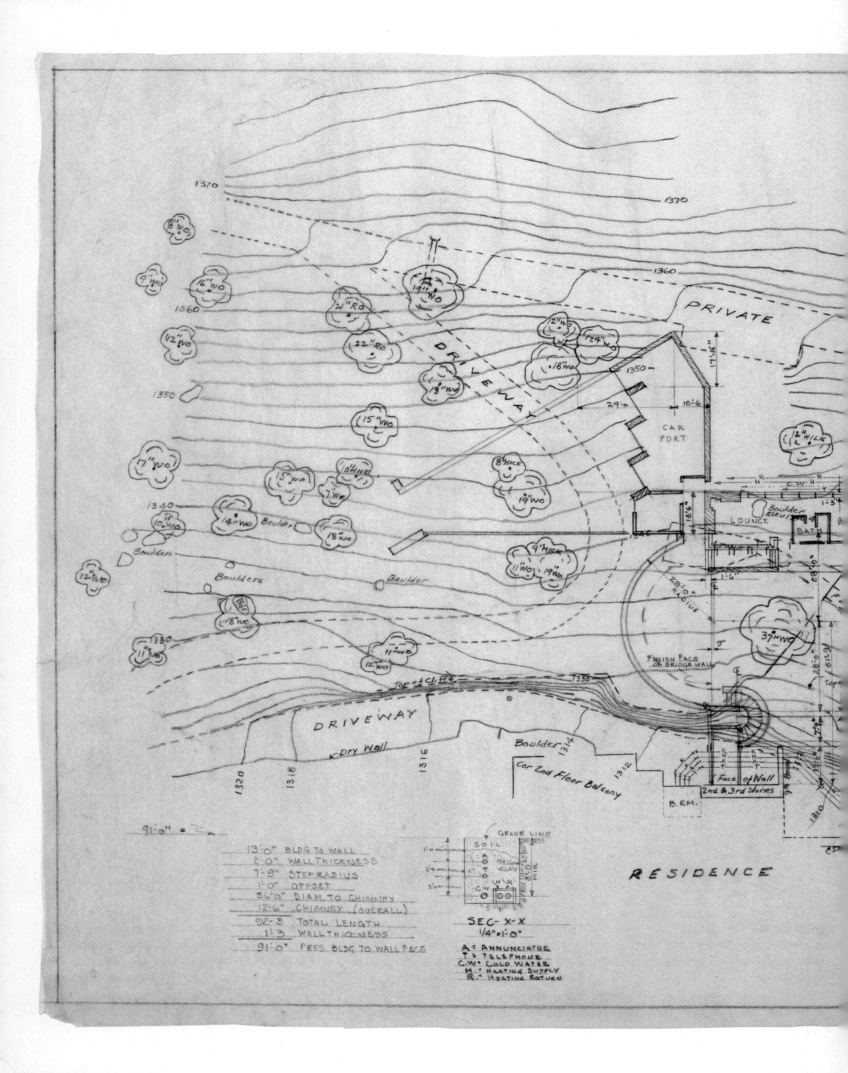

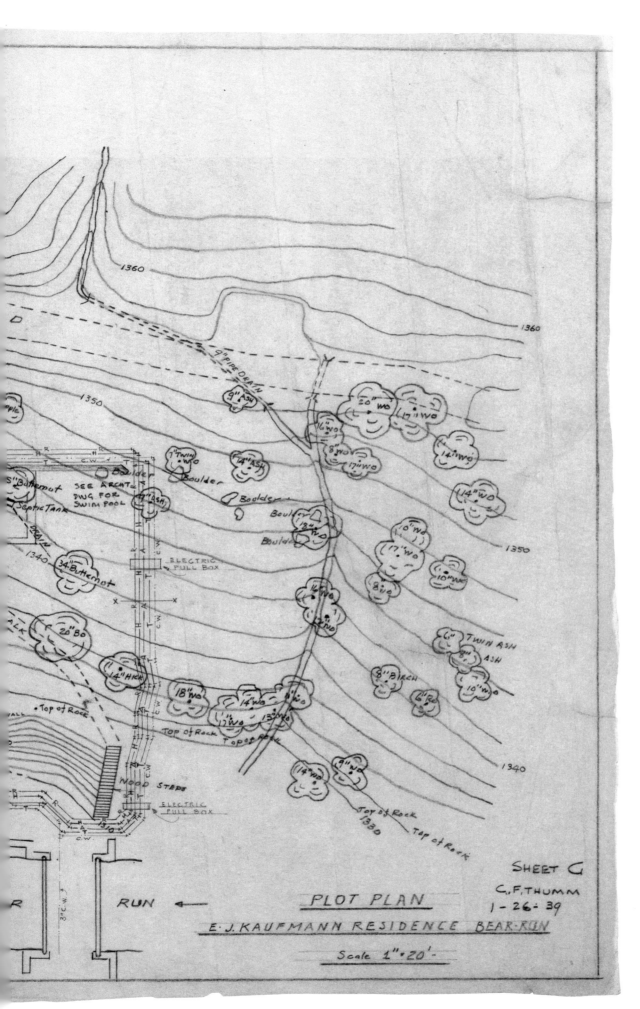

Fallingwater – one of the most famous houses of the twentieth century – is made up of two residences adjacent to a waterfall and river tributary in southeastern Pennsylvania. Construction of the main house took place from 1936 to 1938, while a guest house on the other side of the water was completed in 1939. It's this side of the site that we see in the drawing by Carl F Thumm, an assistant manager at the Pittsburgh department store owned by the client, Edgar J Kaufmann Sr, who was also charged with managing the construction of the house.

The drawing is presumably worked up from a 1935 survey of the area. Thumm has traced the site's trees and topography with a soft pencil. The trees are crudely drawn, but each species is identified and the diameter of each crown is carefully noted. Overlaid onto this existing data is the figure of the guest house and, more importantly, the connecting conduits from the boiler room of the main residence. The pipes, containing water, cables and the heating supply, needed to be organised logistically and their service trench carefully designed for the house to provide the required standards of modern comfort.

pl.7  Frank Lloyd Wright, E J Kaufmann Residence, Fallingwater, Bear Run, Pennsylvania, 1936–39. Pencil on tracing paper, 380 × 550 mm

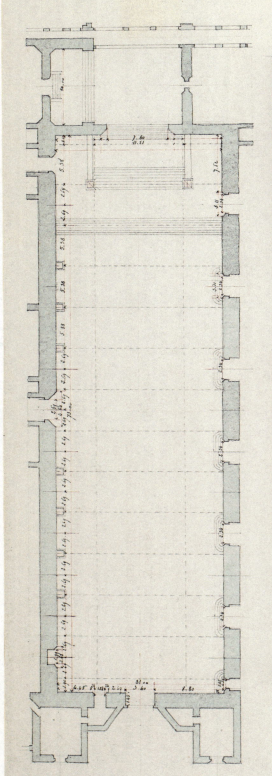

Auguste Gagey was a Paris-based architect educated at the École de Beaux-Arts. After graduating he went into private practice before becoming inspector of works at Reims Cathedral in 1885 – about the same time he made this survey of Westminster Hall. In the centre of the sheet, Gagey gives us a slightly oblique view of the hall, a clear-span space defined by the medieval hammerbeam roof leading to Charles Barry's arched staircase, constructed in 1850 as part of the entrance to his new St Stephen's Hall. Gagey captures a moment in the afternoon, depicting the subtle tonal changes to the walls and floor, while the darkness of the roof space offers a counterpoint to the light of a bright but overcast day. The drawing is flanked by a plan and a section through the hall which record the principal dimensions. Here we can see how architects rely on two different aspects of a survey – the objective gathering of data and the recording of significant experiential moments.

*pl.8* Auguste Gagey, Westminster Hall, Palace of Westminster, *c* 1885. Pencil, pen, ink and watercolour on wove paper, 313 × 479 mm

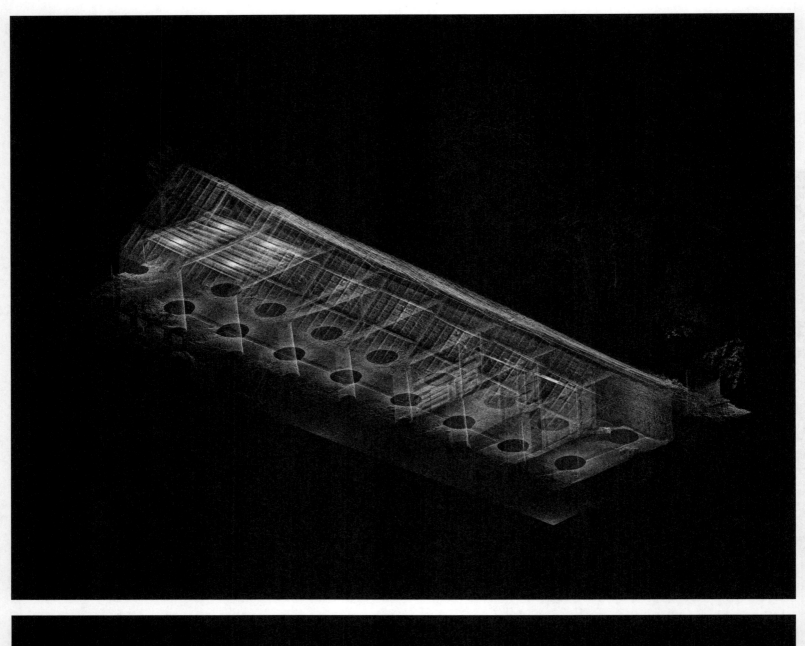
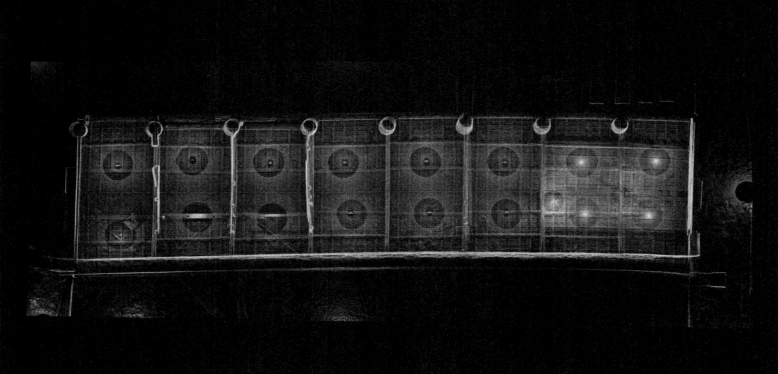

These images, not drawings per se but more like photographs, offer an incredibly detailed 3D survey of one of the buildings at Shatwell Farm, Somerset. 'The Barton', built around 1840 as a milking parlour, is amazingly grand for an agricultural building, with circular stone columns that run along its front edge. Modern mechanised farming rendered the barn obsolete in the 1960s, and it became a dumping ground and timber store for the estate it served.

Over the years the structure liquified, slumping forwards as water exerted pressure on the retaining wall at its back. This project – part experiment, part record, part survey – began in late 2019, when a team embarked on works to try to halt the barn's collapse. A Lidar scanner enabled us to quickly capture the whole building and much of the surrounding site, fixing a version of the building in time.

These images were taken from a virtual model built from 30 individual Lidar scans, stitched together using specialised software. The resulting 3D point cloud is a super-accurate digital representation of the building that can be navigated and inspected from infinite viewpoints. Taking images from these scans is simple, like photographing a whole site from your desk without having to worry about the light conditions. But in translating 3D information (points) into 2D information (pixels), photography becomes a philosophical idea. What's happening is something akin to photography but not quite. They are raster images, but when each coloured pixel in a frame represents a digital point in 3D space, captured by another imaging device, then it forces a reevaluation of the terminology, if not the medium. *Lucas Wilson*

*pl. 9–11*  Zachary Mollica, Jonathan Sellers and Lucas Wilson, 'The Barton', Shatwell Farm, Somerset, 2019. Digital Lidar scan

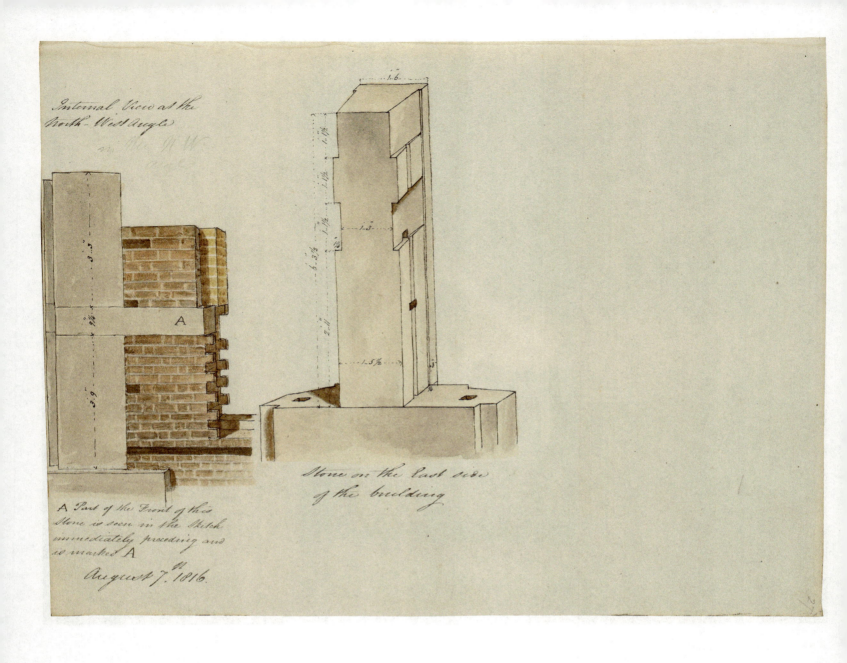

In the summer of 1816 pupils from the office of John Soane made surveys of the Bank of England. The Napoleonic Wars had depleted the bank's revenues, leaving scope only for modest tasks of rebuilding existing offices and making small-scale extensions.

Henry Parke, a pupil of John Soane's between 1814 and 1820, made two different types of drawing during his site visits that summer. There are perspective views of the construction, almost topographic in their panorama of building technology set against the background of London's skyline: pitched roofs and dormers, church spires and chimneys. Rendered in shades of wash, materials become planes of watercolour with little precision in their depiction beyond the play of shadow – a brick wall, for instance, is reduced to a yellow surface.

Counter to this are the measured records of on-site construction. Parke offers an analysis that makes use of several types of orthographic drawings on the same sheet. In addition, he draws in axonometric to show how the blocks for the new stone walls are grooved and connected together with lead, or how the masonry arches are built through centring (the use of timber falsework). In its means of representation, the draughtsmanship is similar to the manuals of building construction that Parke would have been studying at the time.

pl. 12–13   Henry Parke, site progress and record drawings, 7–9 August 1816. Pen and watercolour © Sir John Soane's Museum, London

This painting was made in the early evening in the main square of the medieval town of Gubbio, in central Italy (Perugia). Reached by climbing up narrow winding streets, the Piazza Grande opens out as a belvedere to the southwest, looking across rooftops to the plain below the Apennine foothills. The space is carved out of the medieval city at the top of the hill, surrounded by buildings on three sides, with one long side open and presenting itself to the view. To the west sits the Palazzo dei Consoli with battlements, a tower, and a staircase that cascades onto the piazza and forms an anchoring edge. Seen from below, the palazzo literally holds up the Piazza Grande with a series of vaulted arches beneath it and an anchoring stair to one side, but standing in the piazza, your overwhelming sense is of a piece of space captured and held tautly by the ground of herringbone brick. The brickwork is divided into a pattern of wide bays, with bricks laid in alternating directions so there isn't one primary sense, but instead a cohesive whole. The clay has a slight sheen which reflects light, and on a summer's evening the space glows warmly red. I think of a tenter ground, with the brick as a red cloth stretched tightly. The edge of the piazza is formed by a chest-high brick wall, against which people lean gazing at the view – but until you are standing against it, the view is concealed. Instead, you stand in the space and feel the openness of the ground underfoot and the immensity of the landscape around you.   *Biba Dow*

*pl. 14*   Biba Dow, Piazza Grande, Gubbio, 2012. Watercolour on paper, 138 × 276 mm. Courtesy the architect

It was their slow course along canals and rivers that gave members of the Macartney Embassy, the first diplomatic mission to China (1792–94), time to observe the Chinese landscape from afar. William Alexander, junior draughtsman to the Embassy, made endless sketches and drawings of the mission, with an eye to gauging the market for Lancashire cottons and Indian manufactures in China. Alongside watercolour records of the major diplomatic events, Alexander made drawings of everyday life as seen from his seat on the flat-bottom barge. His views show crowds of villagers and curly-tailed dogs congregating to watch the passing foreigners; domestic objects, clothing and agricultural technology; rice fields, canal infrastructure and buildings. These images provided a wealth of detail about everyday life that was otherwise absent from contemporary accounts.

*pl. 15*  William Alexander, Chinese pagoda, 1793. Pencil on paper, 218 × 178 mm

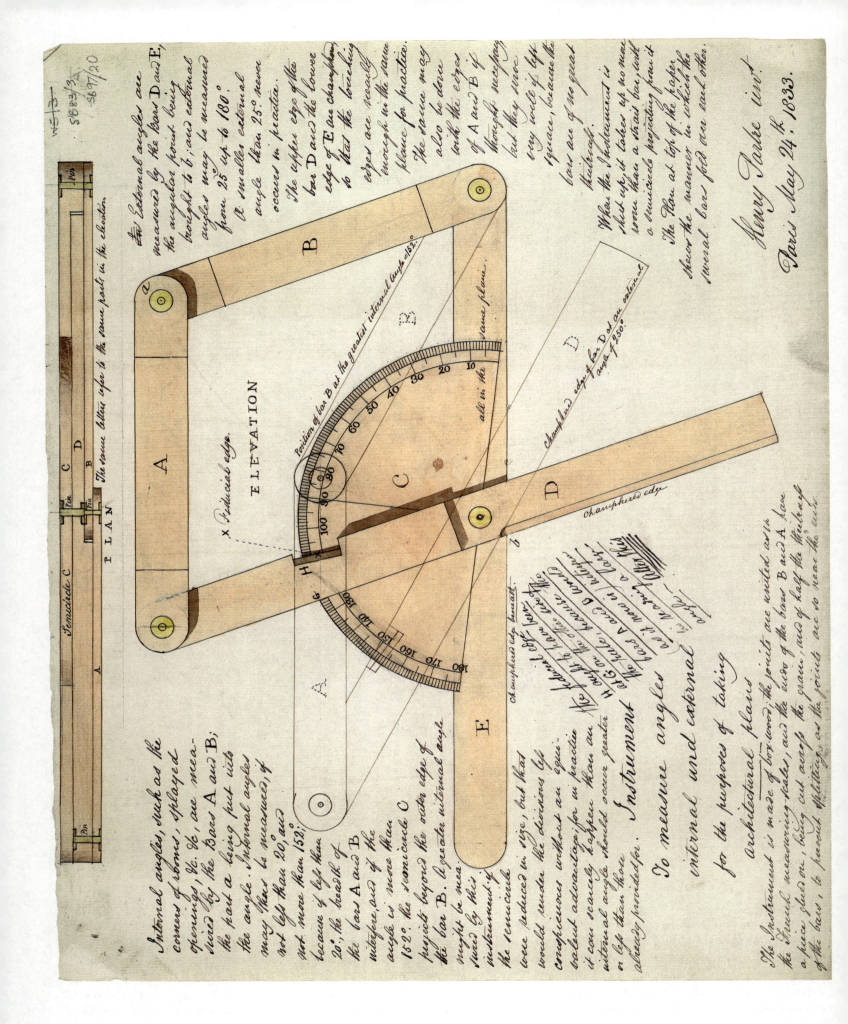

pl. 16  Henry Parke, design for an instrument, 1833. Ink and wash on paper, RIBA Collections

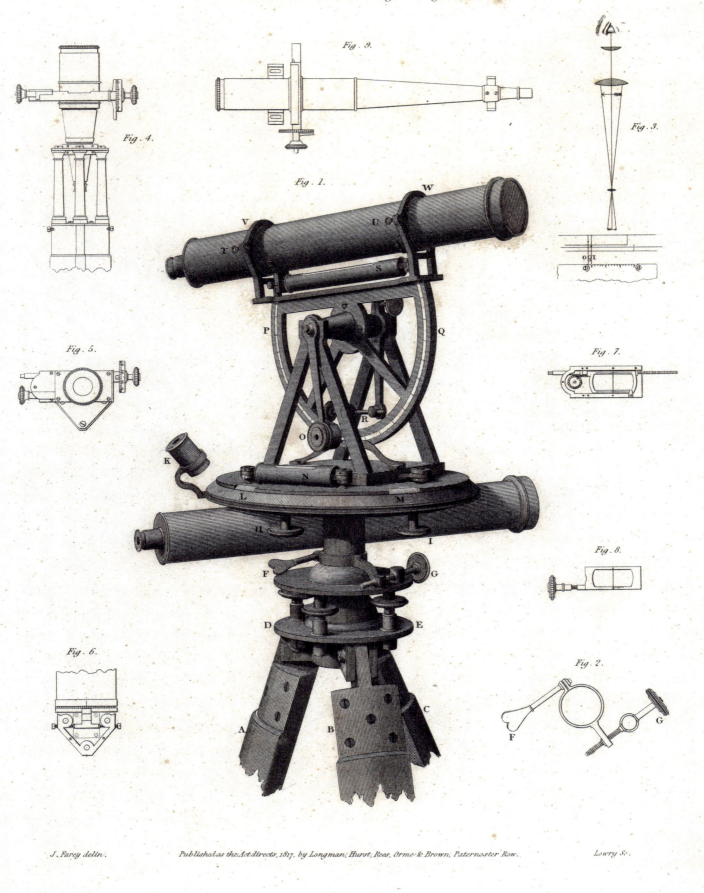

pl. 17 J Boyd (after J Farey), parts and fully assembled portable Theodolite from the American edition of *The cyclopædia, or, Universal dictionary of arts, sciences, and literature*, by Abraham Rees, early nineteenth century. Ink on paper, 275 × 217 mm.
Central Historic Books/Alamy

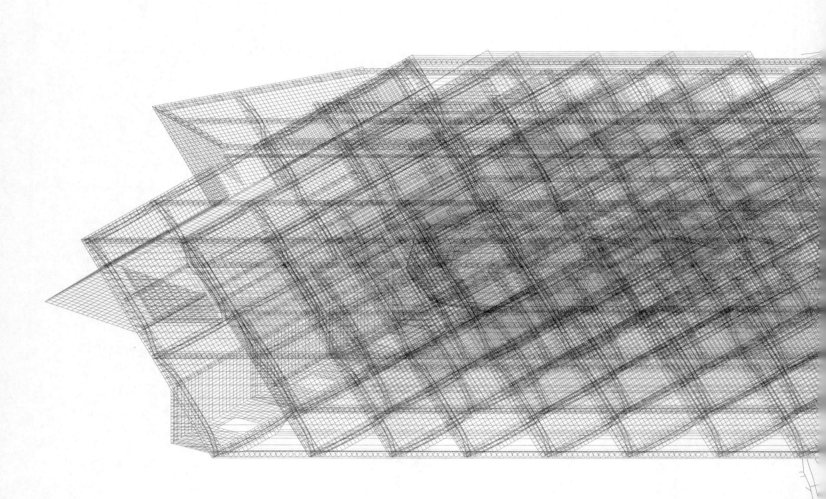

*pl.18* Jann Erhard, Hermes Killer (Studio Tom Emerson, ETH Zurich), survey of the steel reinforcement of the Lion Chambers, from *Glasgow Atlas*, 2014. Courtesy Studio Tom Emerson

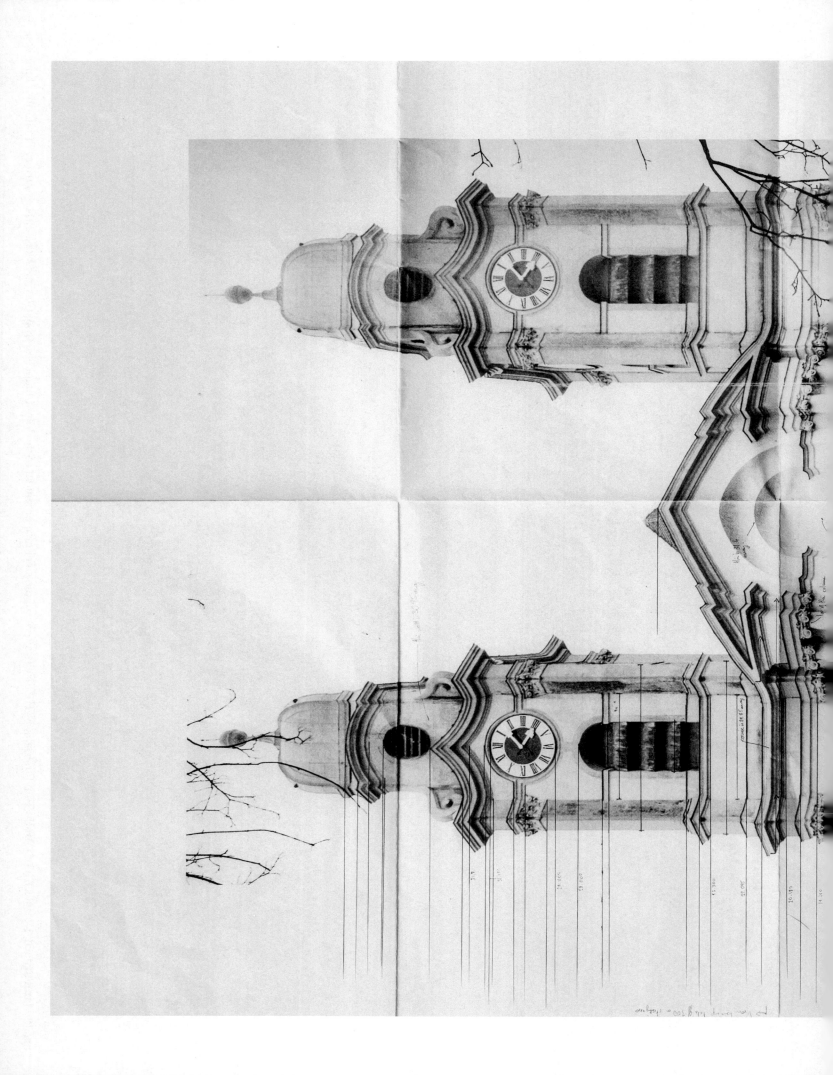

In October 2017 I travelled to Munich to survey Johann Michael Fischer's church of St Michael at Berg am Laim. St Michael is a key example of Fischer's work and of the wider German Rococo movement, and there is no shortage of written and visual information available. I saw the exercise as a way of passively recording the building and of enriching the information that already exists. But it became apparent that the process of measuring a building cannot be passive; it inevitably tells us things that other forms of investigation do not. The 1952 plan and section, prepared by Max Gruber for Norbert Lieb's important book on the Baroque churches of the Danube and Alps, provided a useful template for the notation of measurements. But no elevation drawing of St Michael existed, and so a photograph was used instead – one taken from a distance to reduce the inherent problem of perspective, though it was necessary to remain conscious of this limitation both while making the survey and creating a drawing from it.  *David Valinsky*

pl.19   David Valinsky, St Michael, Berg am Laim, elevation photograph used for survey, 2017. Courtesy the architect

pl.20  Louis François Sébastien Fauvel, measuring Pompey's Pillar, Alexandria, 1789. Pencil and watercolour, 473 × 285 mm

As the range of historical and ethnographic surveys of antique monuments extended in the late eighteenth century, spreading throughout the Mediterranean and the Middle East, painters were engaged as draughtsmen to produce topographical views and make casts alongside young architects from the French Academy in Rome. Louis François Sébastien Fauvel, who had specialised in history painting at the Royal Academy in Paris, accompanied the Comte de Choiseul-Gouffier on his archaeological work in Greece (1780–82), later published as *Voyage pittoresque de la Grèce*. After a second tour of Athens, Fauvel travelled in May 1789 to Alexandria where he purchased objects for the Comte and made drawings of monuments including this watercolour of Pompey's Pillar, built in 297 CE. In his papers, Fauvel describes how he climbed to the summit of the column using a rope that had been flown over and above the monument – hence the prominence of the flying kite on the right side of the picture.

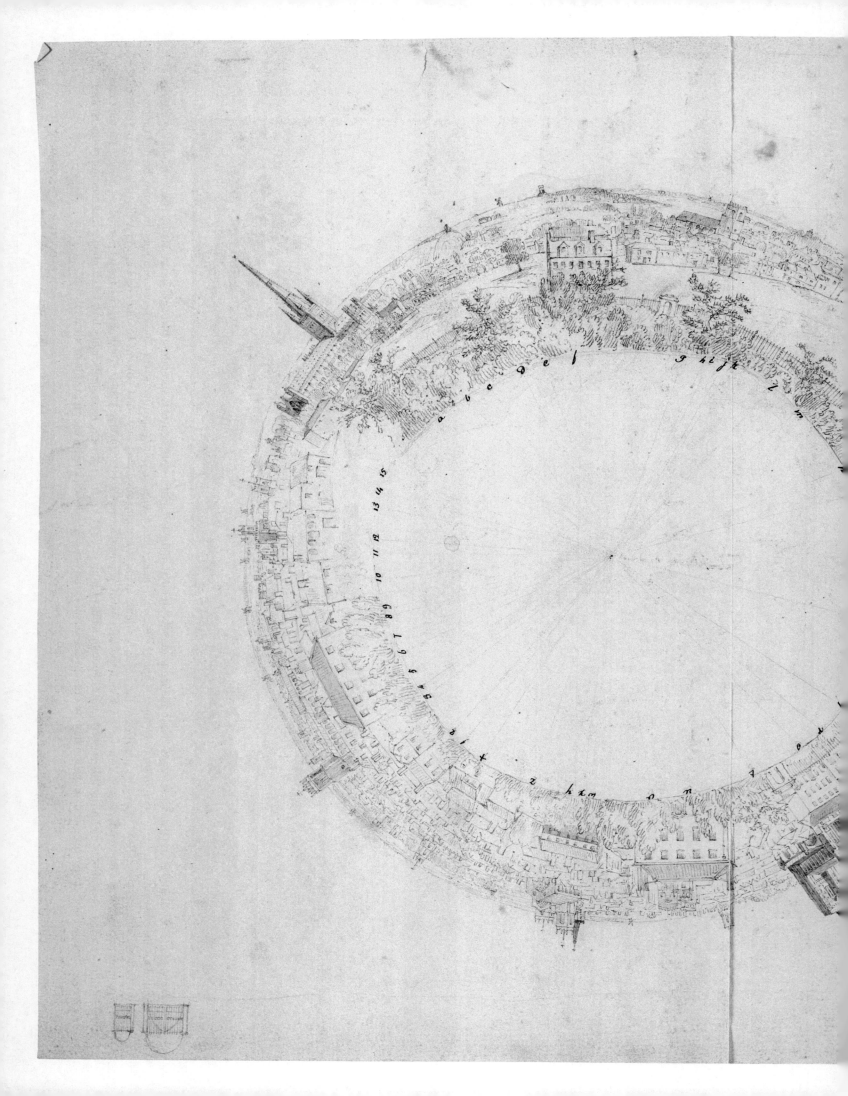

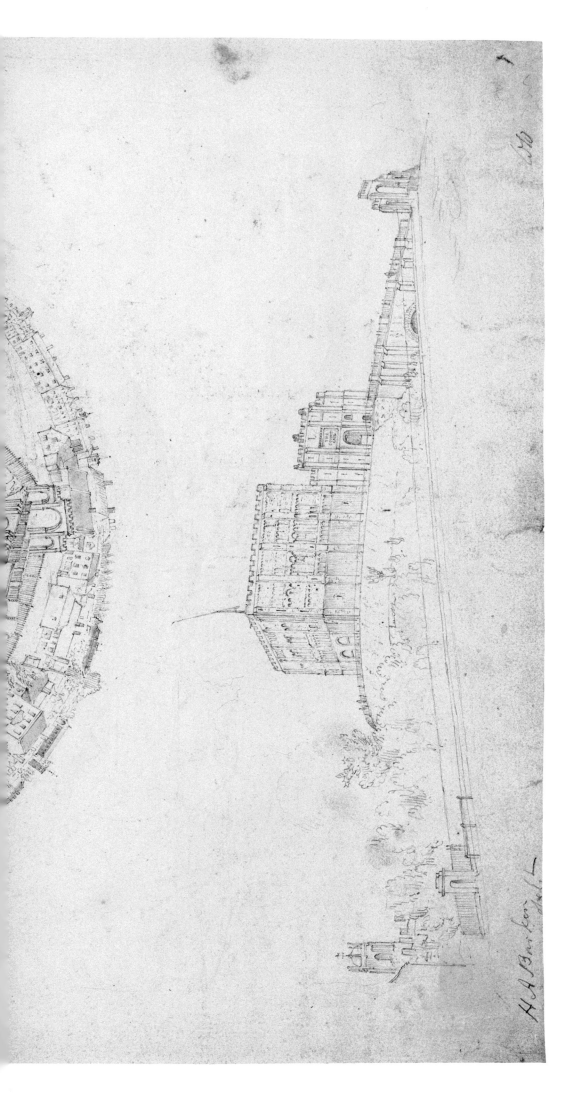

*pl.21* Henry Aston Barker, panoramic view of Norwich and view of Norwich Castle, c 1809. Pencil, pen, ink and wash on wove paper, adhered to backing sheet, 443 × 330 mm

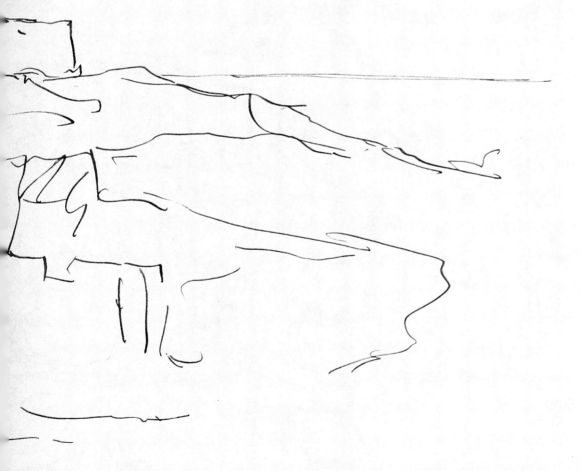

pl.22   Hans Hollein, perspective of Hopi village, Second Mesa, 1960. Black ink on wove paper, 329 × 418 mm

This drawing was made with a chinagraph pen over the course of a holiday afternoon. It started out roughly, as a quick sketch, but time stretched out as more people filled the page. I like using chinagraph as it can be sensitive to great softness and also very dark lines. I like its texture – it is a very direct medium and you cannot alter its mark once it is on the page, and so it forces you to look carefully and commit to the line you are making.

The view is from a first-floor terrace that bridges over the old wooden entrance gates to the palazzina of the Tonnara di Scopello in Sicily, a medieval walled estate once supported by tuna fishing. The Tonnara sits on a picturesque lagoon, and today its pitted concrete causeway has become a public beach. At night it is home to visitors staying in the palazzina and in the old fishermen's houses that line the slopes around the bay. When I made this drawing, 80-year-old Giovanni – bright eyed, leathery skinned, wiry and fit – was still living in one of them. He was always to be found sitting beneath the fig tree that can be seen in the middle distance of the drawing, having worked all his life in this place. I love the way that this former working space has become a multi-generational public realm. It is as busy as a town square where people, quite unguarded in their demeanour, chat and relax in groups and pairs; different characters emerge. A parapet ledge of old mismatched patterned cement tiles in the foreground is a typical Sicilian detail. *Stephanie Macdonald*

pl.23 Stephanie Macdonald, Concrete Beach, Tonnara di Scopello, 2013. Chinagraph pen on paper, 297 × 420 mm. Courtesy the architect

pl. 24  Arata Isozaki, *Re-ruined Hiroshima*, 1968. Ink and gouache with cut-and-pasted gelatin silver print on gelatin silver print, 352×937 mm © 2020 MoMA / Scala, Florence

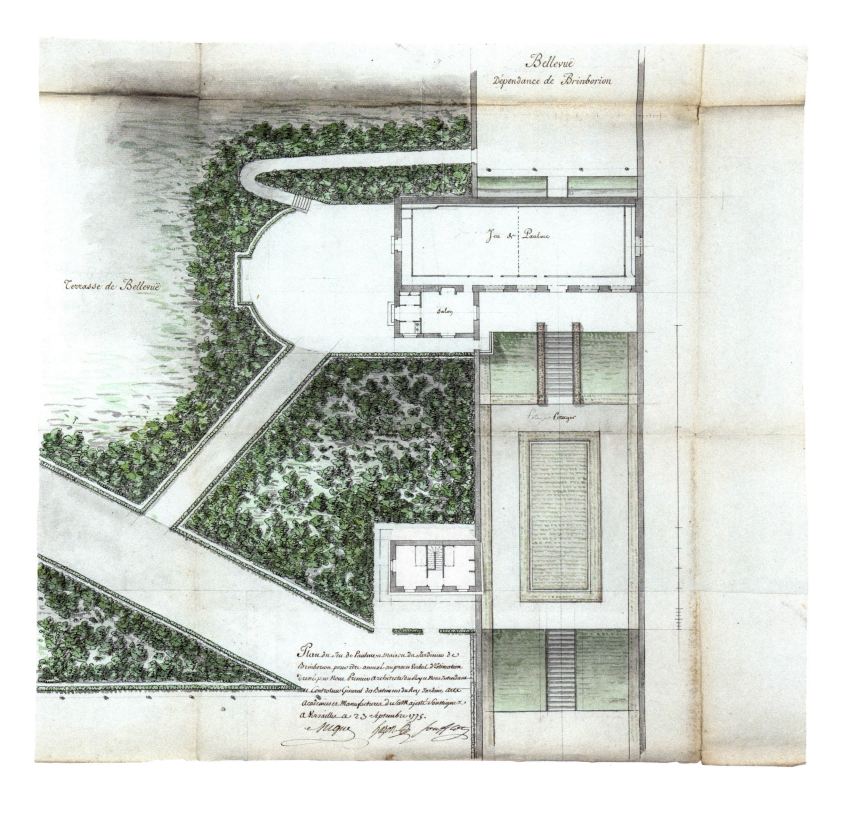

'Plan of the Jeu de Paulme and Gardener's House at Brimborion to be annexed to the *proces Verbal d'Annexation* drawn up by ourselves, the *premier Architecte du Roy* in attendance to the *Controleur General des Batimens du Roy, Jardins, Arts, Academies et Manufactures* of his Majesty. Undersigned at Versailles on the 23rd September 1775.  *Mique, Hazon, Soufflot*'

*pl. 25*   Richard Mique, ground plan of Jeu de Paume, gardener's house and terrace walks, 1775. Pen, ink and watercolour on watermarked laid paper, 490 × 475 mm

Route 91 passes through Las Vegas. Denise Scott Brown's photographs, taken on research trips with students, created a catalogue of the city's suburban sprawl and emergence as an 'automobile city'. On the trips, fieldwork consisted of ten days spent gathering maps and aerial photographs of the existing city and comparing them against oral histories and early photographs to analyse changes to the urban fabric. Students photographed the Strip and Fremont Street, the two major thoroughfares at the time, splicing together panoramas from individual shots taken at regular intervals. Films were made by attaching cameras to the front of a car and driving down the Strip. Altogether, the students' survey resulted in texts, photographs, video and audio tapes, charts, maps, drawings, two songs, a cake and a book. These images documented the asphalt, the empty parking lots and the signage of the city's casinos and churches, hotels and bars.

As inscribed within *Learning from Las Vegas*, which Denise Scott Brown published with Robert Venturi and Steven Izenour in 1972, the photographs were a part of a larger argument about modern architecture that distinguished between two different building types – those which are expressive in form or volume ('a duck') and those which use ornament or symbols to describe their purpose ('a decorated shed').

By taking the territory of Las Vegas seriously, the survey became a central part of the radical reconfiguration of architecture, focusing on the everyday residues of modern life.

*pl. 26–27*  Denise Scott Brown, the Strip, Las Vegas, 1965. Courtesy the architect

Climbing and surveying the ruins of Rome was potentially dangerous, and there are reports of near-fatal accidents involving falls from height. George Wightwick, who would be employed by Soane on his return from Italy, advised students 'not to risk [their] neck in measuring, for the thousandth time, a Roman ruin'. An abundance of archaeological and antiquarian surveys had been carried out in seventeenth-century Rome, each made with increasing intensity and precision. But by the mid-eighteenth century, a younger generation had become critical of these earlier surveys, which sometimes showed buildings without their post-antique extensions or, conversely, with their decoration restored.

New surveys were therefore required. As Robert Adam explained in a 1755 letter to his brother from Rome, the way to do it was to make all the measurements anew. But taking accurate measurements was no easy matter. If an observer stood on a tall ladder resting against a building, they could gaze up at an entablature and make a sketch and estimate distances based on measurements taken at ground level. But with this upwards gaze came a parallax distortion in the eye. For this reason, scaffolding – which allowed the observer to stand right next to the entablature – became a site-specific art-form, adapted to the specific dimensions and requirements of the monument to be studied. George Ledwell Taylor and Edward Cresy, authors of a comprehensive survey of Rome, later published as *The architectural antiquities of Rome* (1821–22), benefited from an existing structural frame erected to support the Arch of Titus during its restoration, stripping away the accretions of a medieval tower (see page 55). John Goldicutt, an architect better known for his surveys than his buildings, had to improvise, and measured the Temple of Vespasian from a cradle cantilevered out from the entablature and accessed from the ground by two ladders.

*pl. 28*   John Goldicutt, Temple of Vespasian, Rome, scaffolded for measuring, December 1816. Pencil on paper, 245 × 180 mm

230

SD99/23 ③

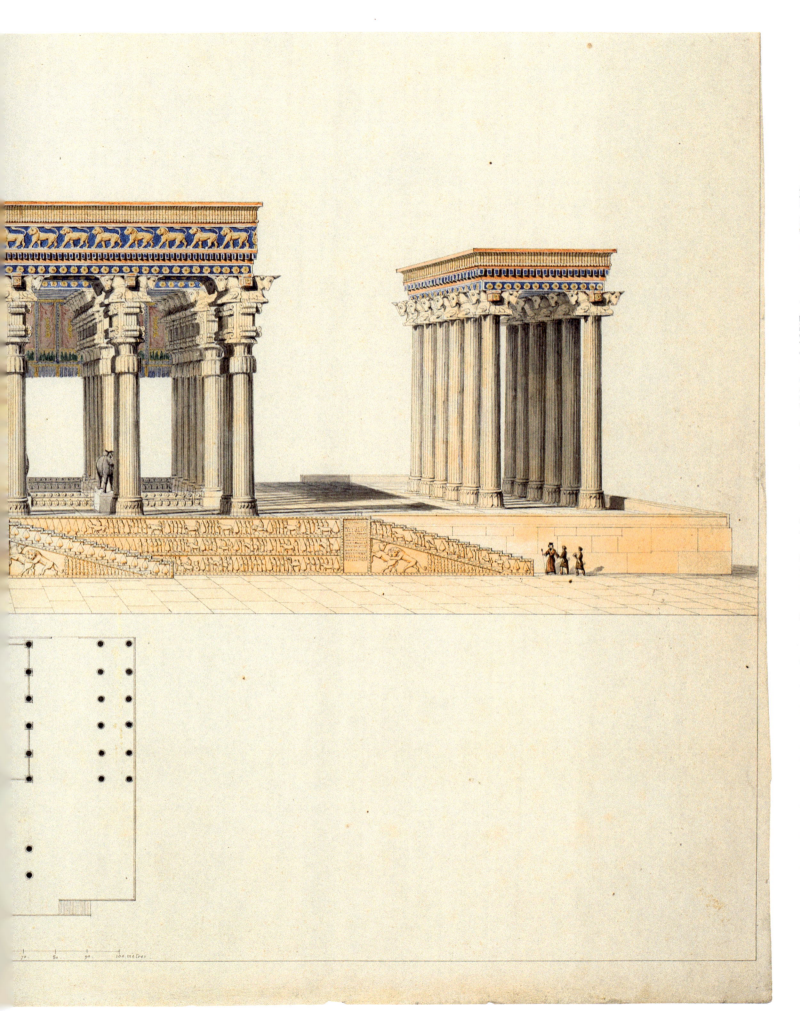

pl. 29   Pascal Coste, Palace of Darius, Persepolis, c 1840. Pen, ink watercolour and gold ink on laid Whatman paper, 315 × 508 mm

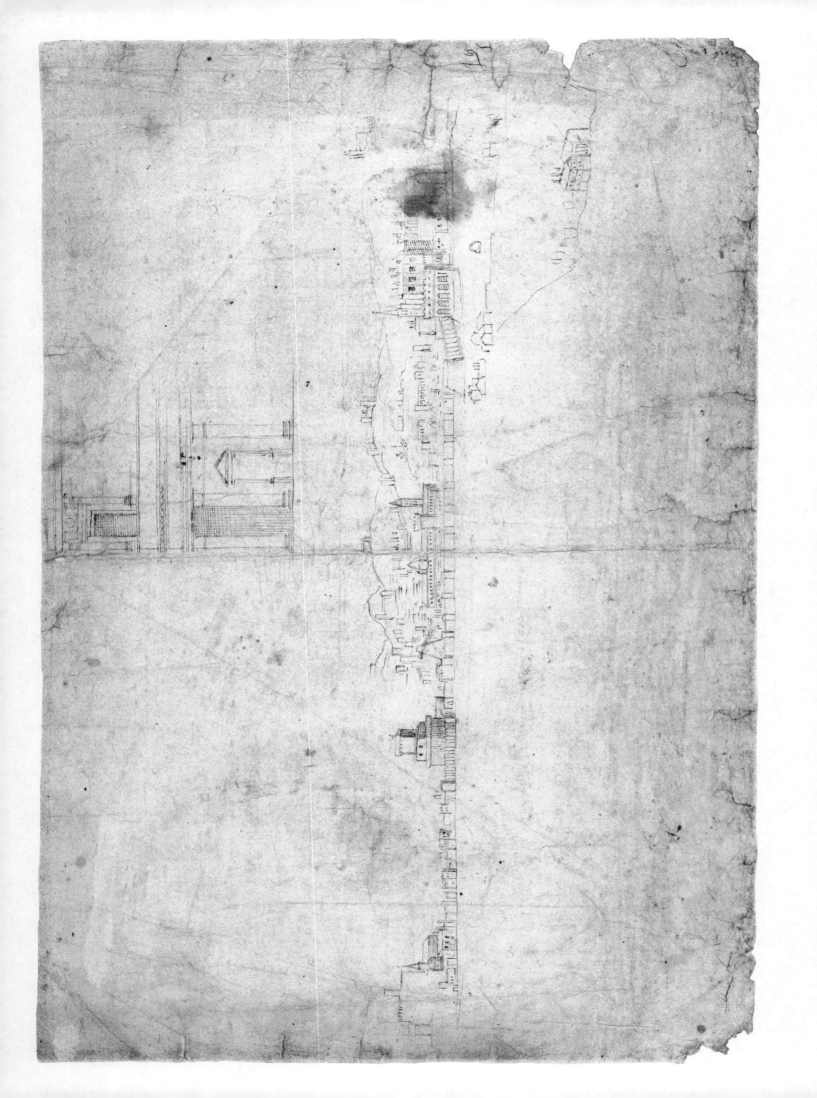

*pl.30* Anonymous (after Raphael), *view of Rome and the Vatican, and interior detail of the Pantheon*, c 1500–50, ink on paper, 286 × 413 mm. University Library Salzburg

*pl.31* Attributed to J Carrey, *view of Athens*, from *Dessins des sculptures du Parthénon* (Henri Omont, editor), 1898. Ink on paper. Heidelberg University Library

# KARNAC

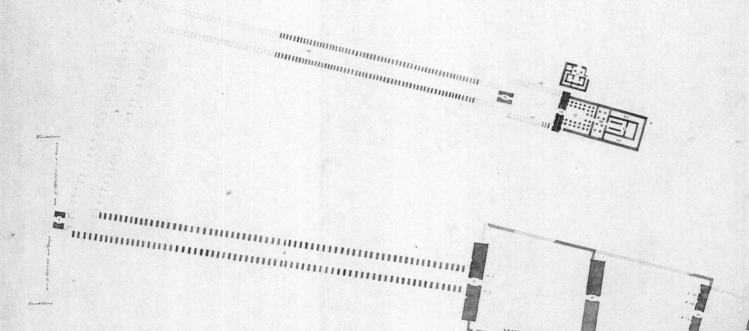

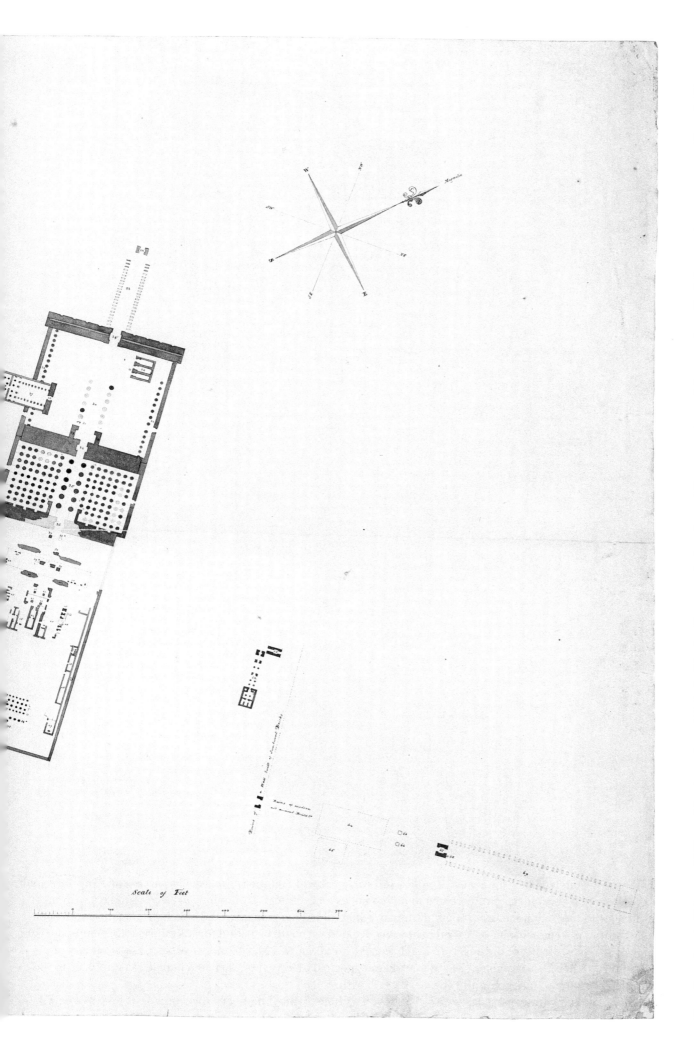

Over four days in February 1819, working from dawn till dusk, Charles Barry made drawings of the excavations of the complex of buildings and monuments at Karnak. He spent the first day and a half surveying and preparing a rough 'general plan', which was then redrawn to produce this 'best' copy. The whole experience made a deep impression on the young architect. In a diary entry he notes: 'This is certainly the finest thing in Egypt for though it cannot be judged by the strict rules of architectural proportions and symmetry yet when in the midst of such a vast assemblage of columns the effect it produced upon me was the most impressive I ever experienced and one feels inclined to look over the many inconsistencies that appear upon investigation of it in detail when it is considered as a whole.'

*pl.32* Charles Barry, Karnak, Egypt, 1819. Black ink on cartridge paper, with sepia wash, 533 × 838 mm

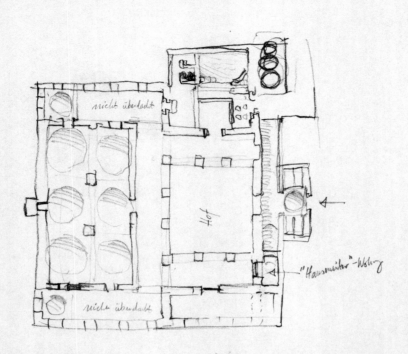

'Next year, there will be a civil war in Yemen. Please lend me the money so I can go now,' I had the wit to ask my parents after my first year in architecture school. I didn't know that this journey would come to define me as an architect. I'd not long arrived in Sana'a with my travel companion, Holger Sulitze, when we met an aristocratic Italian man who resided in a palace in the old city – his father had been the private physician of the last sultan of Yemen in the 1960s. Somehow, he decided we could be useful for his efforts to promote tourism, and he provided us with a jeep and a driver to cross the desert to reach the Queen of Sheba's Marib and, beyond it, the great city of Shibam in the Wadi Hadramaut. From there, we stumbled, literally, from one magical place to the next on a journey that took us to the coast, to the green hills of Arabia Felix, and to the mountains in the rugged north.

Sketching throughout the trip, I felt a strange paradox which has stayed with me: while I had been drawing for as long as I could remember, would drawing help me to be a good architect? Or is my facility in drawing – the lack of resistance – a problem? I was fixated on the idea that drawing should be an act of humility. I believed that as an architectural novice I should avoid formulaic abstraction

and rhetorical analysis in my sketches. I felt that drawing a building should almost be an act of worship, that it should involve complete and unreserved appreciation. According to my logic, using hard lead ranging from 4H to 6H would create a resistance that would force me to look more precisely, with the use of a hard pencil favouring cold objectivity over a superficial painterly effect. For me, objectivity meant that I would rely mainly on contour lines for the structure of the drawing. In my imagination, continuous contour lines worked like magic circles in which one could entrap buildings.

Drawing felt different in 1993. It was before the internet and drawing still retained its original authority as a technique for documentation. Knowing that there was the possibility of a civil war, I felt a strange sense of urgency. I was aware that I might never be able to return, and that some of the buildings I sketched during my journey might be destroyed in the near future. *Thomas Padmanabhan*

*pl. 33–34* Thomas Padmanabhan, sketchbook from Yemen, alley in Thula and Al-Ismail Mosque, 1993. Courtesy the architect

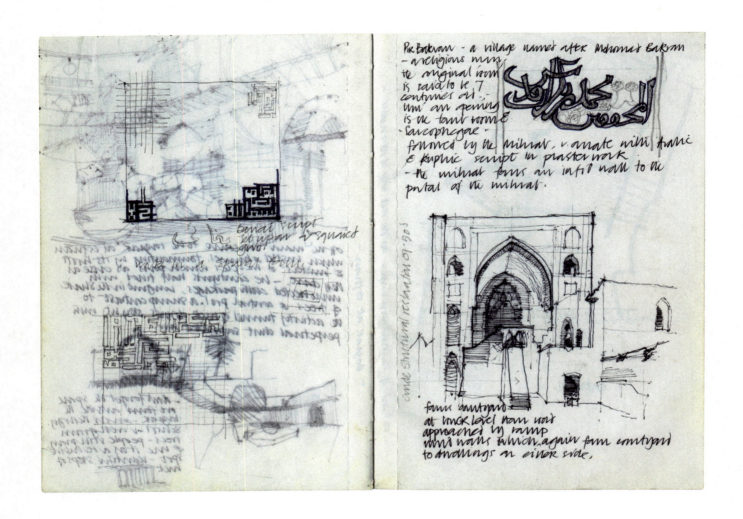

What's different about this sketchbook, I see now if I open the page, is that it was made at a time when one had time. There was no planning just what caught the eye or mind. And there is not much evidence of the months involved, only a hint of the daily struggle, with a lot of travelling across these pages. They describe the village and the mausoleum of Pir Bakran, with some observations about the threshold and the Kufic script on the inner walls of the courtyard. The first pages of the book reflect a rapid passage south with my then girlfriend Sue Francis. We travelled the first month together, driving out from London on a motorcycle, then our paths diverged when she returned to start her diploma at the Architectural Association. After getting Sue to her plane, I caught up with Andy Thorne and we spent the rest of the year travelling. Somewhat by chance we attended the Second International Conference of Architects,

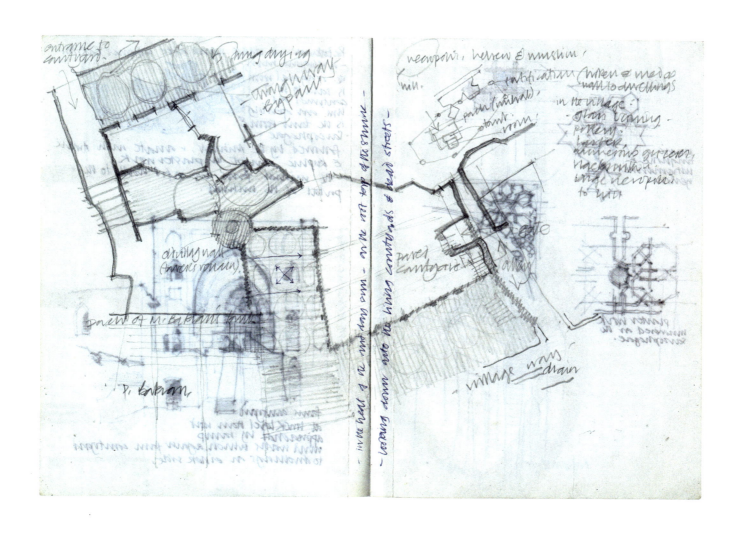

held in the Tent City that the Shah had erected just outside Persepolis to celebrate the 2500th anniversary of the founding of the Achaemenid Kingdom (Khomeini, by the way, called it the 'devil's festival'). There, we found ourselves among the architectural great and the good: Derek Walker, O M Ungers, Nadir Adalan, Hassan Fathy, James Stirling, Georges Candilis, Josep Lluís Sert, Moshe Safdie, Paolo Soleri and Buckminster Fuller. Andy and I – about to embark on our surveying of nomadic settlements – found it surreal.
*Eric Parry*

pl. 35–36   Eric Parry, Iran sketchbook, 1974. Pencil, black and blue pen on paper. Courtesy the architect

Plan du Saint Sépulcre à Jérusalem.

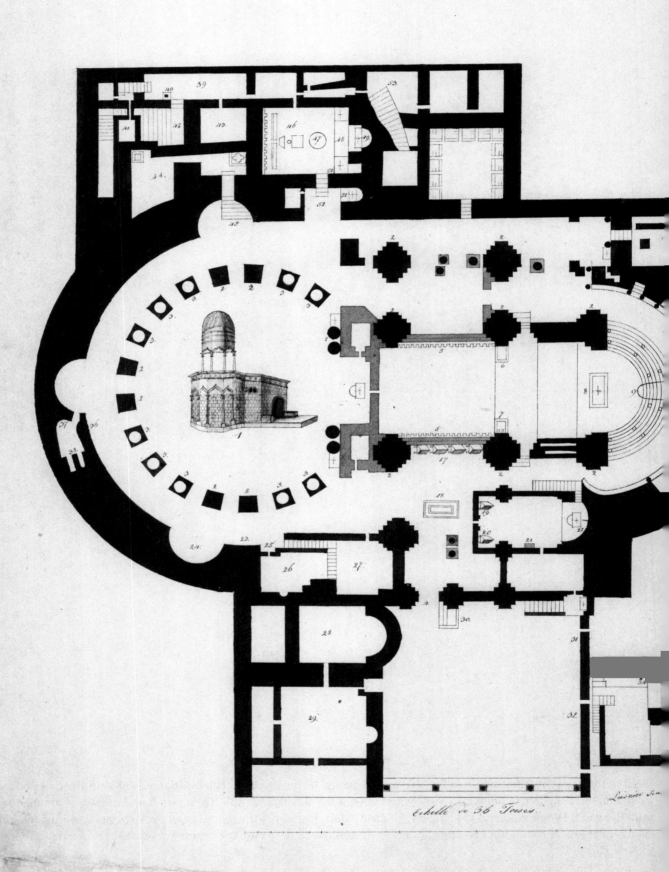

Echelle de 36 Toises.

Le Saint Sepulcre. 2. Bases de l'Eglise 3 Colonnes de l'Eglise
Port de l'Eglise. 5 Chœur des Grecs. 6 Siège du Patriarche. 7. Siège du
Patriarche d'Alexandrie. 8. Grand autel des Grecs. 9. Siège du Patriarche de
Rome. 10 Chapelle du titre de la S.te Croix. 11. Lieu de la division des vêtemens de J.C.
Chapelle de la colonne de l'impropere 13. la prison de J.C. 14. Autel du bon larron
Chapelle de S.te Helene. 16. Lieu de l'invention de la S.te Croix 17 Sépulcre de plusieurs rois
reines de Jerusalem. 18. Pierre de l'onction 19. Sépulcre du roi Baudouin 20 Sépulcre
roi Godefroi de Bouillon 21. Sepulcre de Melchisédeck 22. Fente du M.t Calvaire
Habitation des Abyssins. 24. Lieu où étoient les Apôtres 25 Escalier pour monter chez
armeniens 26. Chambre haute des Armeniens 27. Chambre du Portier des Goths.
Tour du clocher 29. Eglise des Grecs. 30 Station des Turcs 31 Eglise des Goths
Eglise des Armeniens 33. Où N.S. fut mis sur la croix 34. Fente de la Montagne
Où J.C. fut crucifié. 36. Habitation des Goths 37. Habitation des Syriens.
Sepulcre de Nicodeme et de Joseph d'Arimathie 39. Le grand réfectoire. 40.
iterne de S.te Helene. 41. Habitation des religieux 42. Où l'on fait la lessive
pour la Sacristie. 43. P.tit refectoire de la communauté 44. Citerne commune
Entrée pour aller a la Citerne commune. 46 Le chœur des Freres mineurs. 47
Lieu ou la vrai Croix fut reconnue 48. Lieu ou apparut J.C. a sa mère après sa
surrection 49 Grand Autel. 50. Autel ou l'on conserve des Reliques 51 Cha-
lle de la Madeleine 52. Entrée du couvent de S.t François. 53 Passage pour
allez à d'autres habitations.

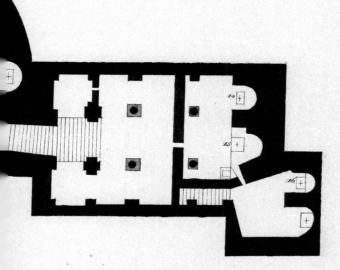

pl. 37  Nicolas Auguste Leisonier, Church of the Holy Sepulchre, Jerusalem, c 1825. Pen and black ink on wove paper, 410 × 495 mm

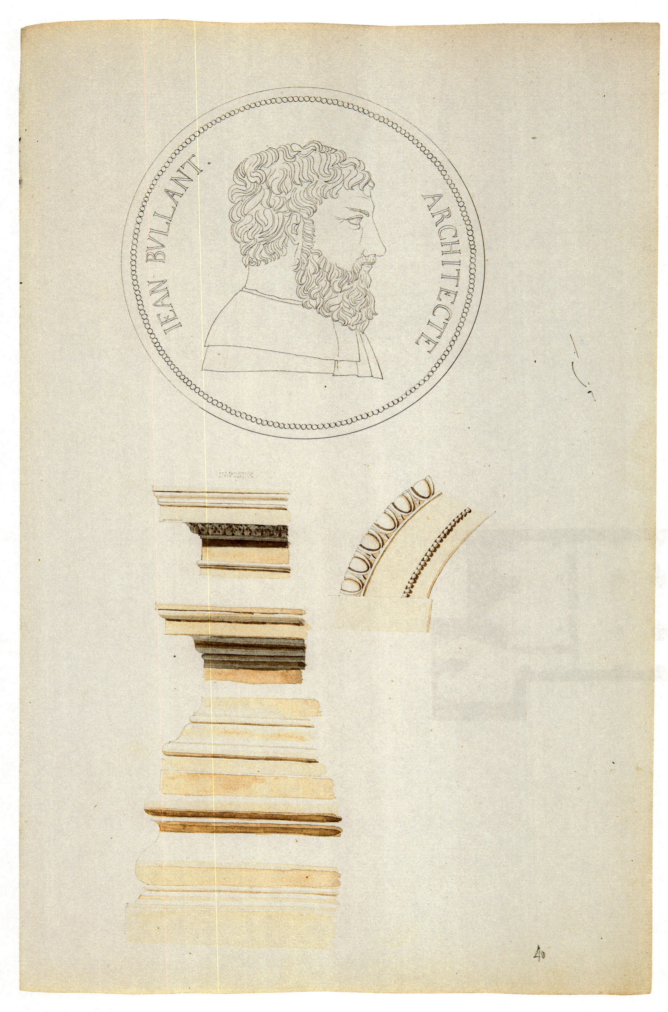

*pl. 38* Charles Percier, medallion design for 'Jean Bullant Architecte', with portrait profile mouldings, 1800–50. Pen, ink and coloured washes, 370 × 250 mm

*pl. 39* Charles Percier, plan for 'Aubege [sic] sur la route de Florence', external elevation: 'Sepulcre de JC'; panel of candelabra ornament, 1800–50. Pen, ink and coloured washes, 370 × 250 mm

*pl. 40* Giovanni Battista Montano, Roman basilica building (half-elevation and section), *c* 1600. Brown ink and brown wash, 140 × 138 mm

*pl. 41* Giovanni Battista Montano, tomb of C Publicius Bibulus (half-elevation and section), *c* 1600. Brown ink and brown wash, 150 × 140 mm

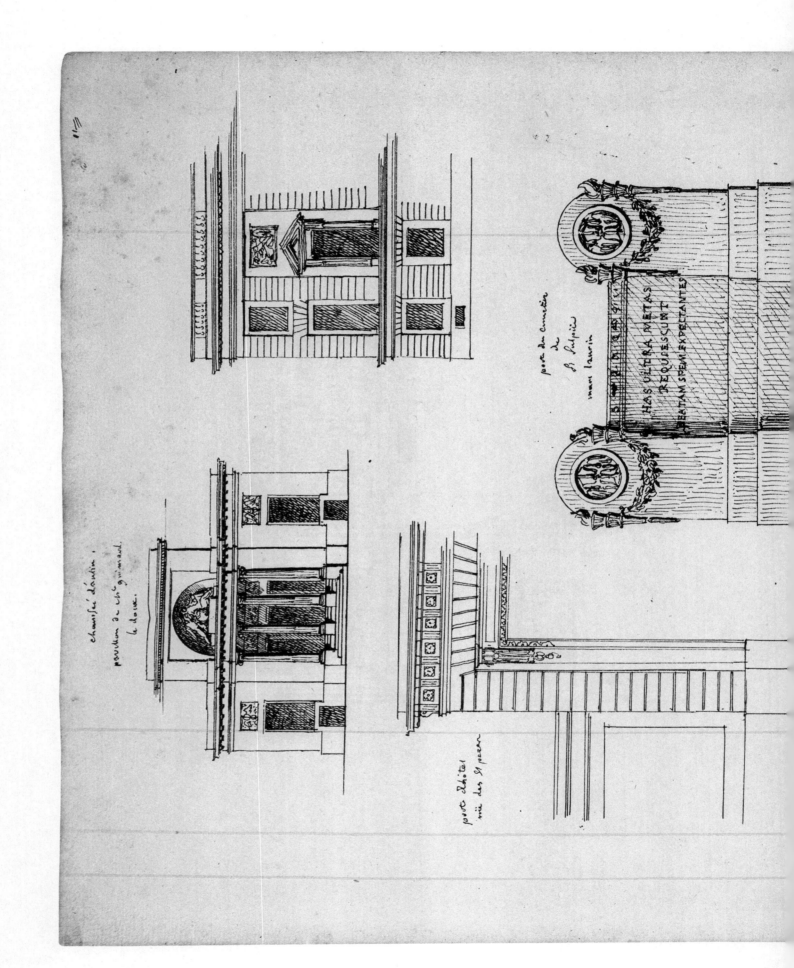

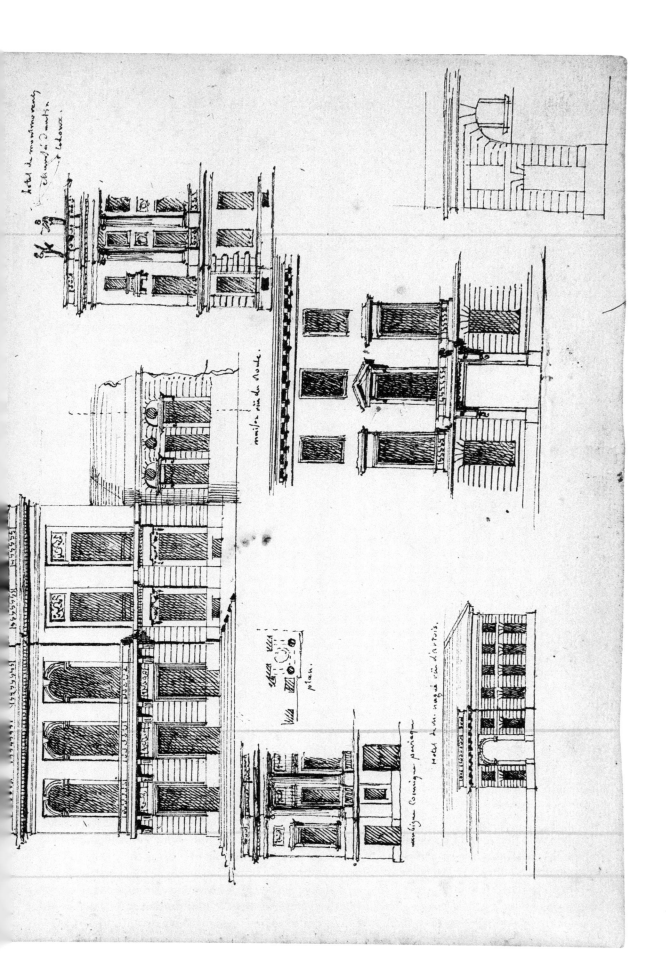

*pl. 42* Pierre Adrien Paris, sketchbook of architectural detail, ornament and furnishings, 1770. Pen and ink, 370×250 mm

A student of Charles Percier, André Châtillon won the Grand Prix de Rome in 1809 – on his seventh attempt – which enabled him to stay on at the French Academy in Rome until 1813. This survey is indicative of the concerns of a *pensionnaire* during their time in Italy. Key dimensions of a building (portal, entablature, pediment) have been carefully measured and drawn assuredly with a straightedge, while decorative detail is more easily applied, sketched freehand with shade and relief suggested by a careful use of ink wash.

The album containing these drawings was bound by the great-nephew of Charles Percier in 1888. When studied as a whole, it offers an extraordinary example of an architect's miscellany of references, including Châtillon's original design drawings for built works, studies made while in Rome, prints from iconic literature of antique and Renaissance architecture, sketches of northern French medieval monuments, and exercises from his time at the École des Beaux-Arts. Châtillon would later become the architect of the Department of the Seine, responsible for building the Marché des Patriarches in Paris and the Notre Dame de la Nativité in Bercy.

*pl. 43*  André Châtillon, pediment studies from an album of architectural drawings, *c* 1814–30. Pencil and ink on paper, 315 × 275 mm

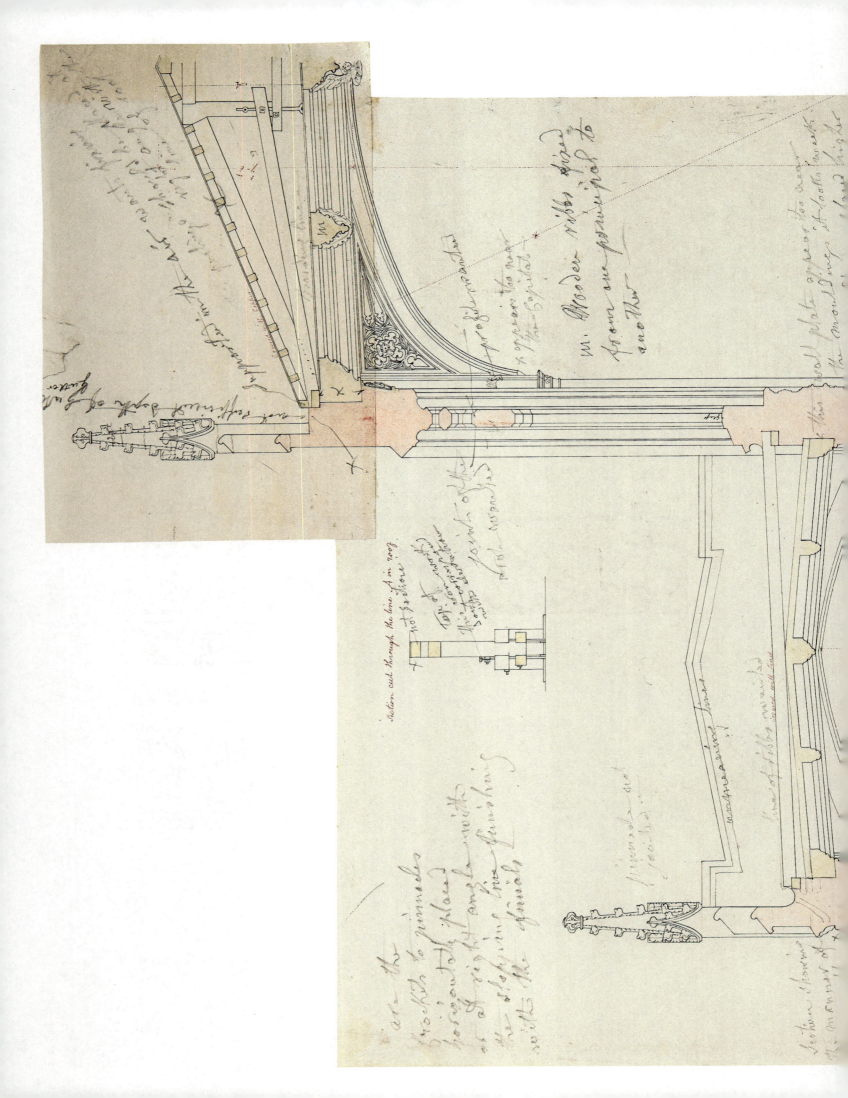

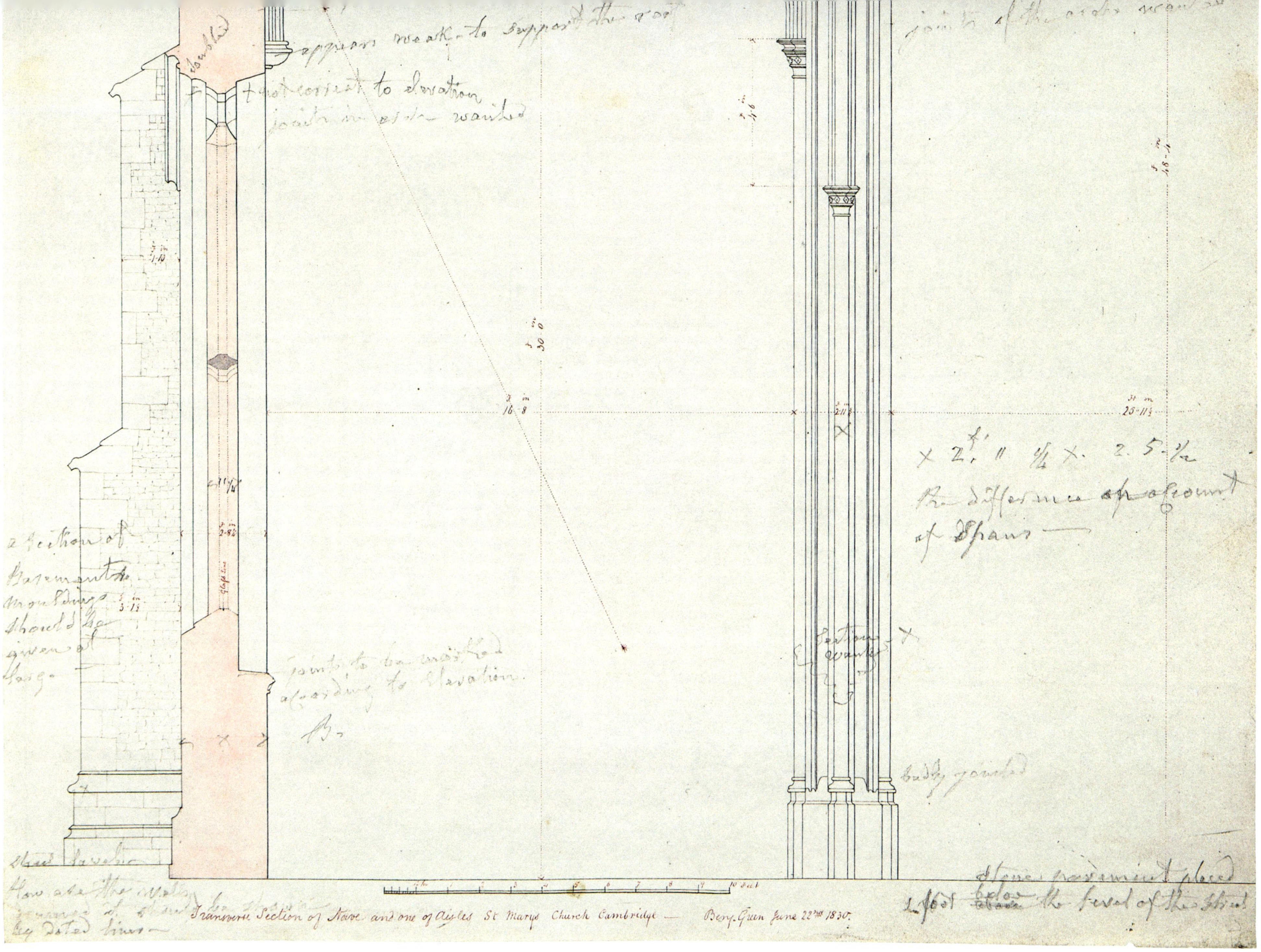

*pl.44* AWN Pugin, St Mary's Church, Cambridge, 1830. Pencil, pen and ink and pink, yellow and grey wash, 590 × 375 mm

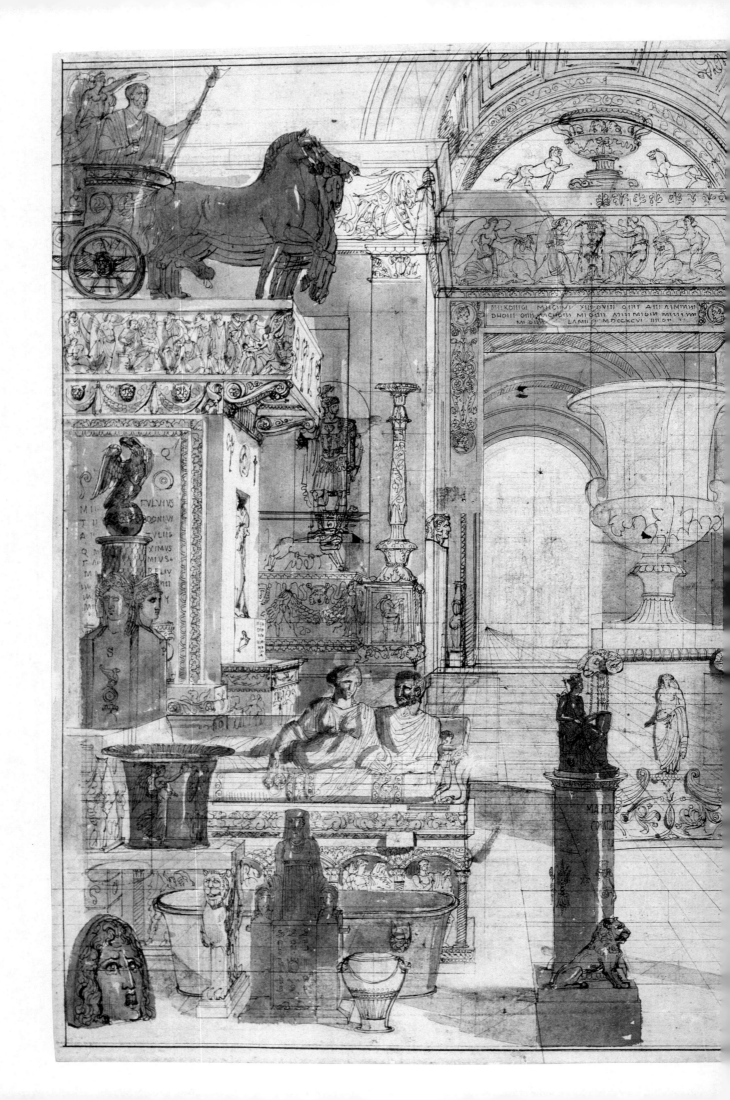

pl. 45  Charles Percier, preparatory drawing for a Muséum Idéal, 1796. Pen, ink, wash and bodycolour on reverse, 457 × 584 mm

pl. 46 Jean-Augustin Renard, study of a Corinthian capital in white marble, 1777. Lithograph, 440×335 mm

*pl. 47* George Niemann, detail of arch, Hadrian's Gate, *c* 1890. Pen, ink and wash on wove paper laid on backing sheet, 502 × 387 mm

*pl. 48*  Eugène-Emmanuel Viollet-le-Duc, tomb of Bishop *Philippe de Dreux*, *c* 1874. Gouache and red ink on laid paper, 283 × 195 mm

*pl. 49–52* The Street Observation Society (Rojo Kansatsu Gakkai, or ROJO), manhole covers (Mantua, Rome, Milan). Courtesy ROJO

Zurich is familiar in plan, surveyed by municipal authorities in maps and cadastral plans to show its urban development. In this view from above we can see the city's dense historic core surrounded by the hillside villas of the nineteenth-century bourgeoisie, a morphology that changes in the twentieth century with the apartment blocks and railways in the inner city and the suburban sprawl of logistics centres and slip roads that serve the surrounding hinterland.

    Less familiar is the city in section, a drawing that can, through its vertical depiction, synthesise the different scales of the city: its buildings, landscape and infrastructure alongside the activities of daily life. If we turn to this contemporary city, what do a kitchen

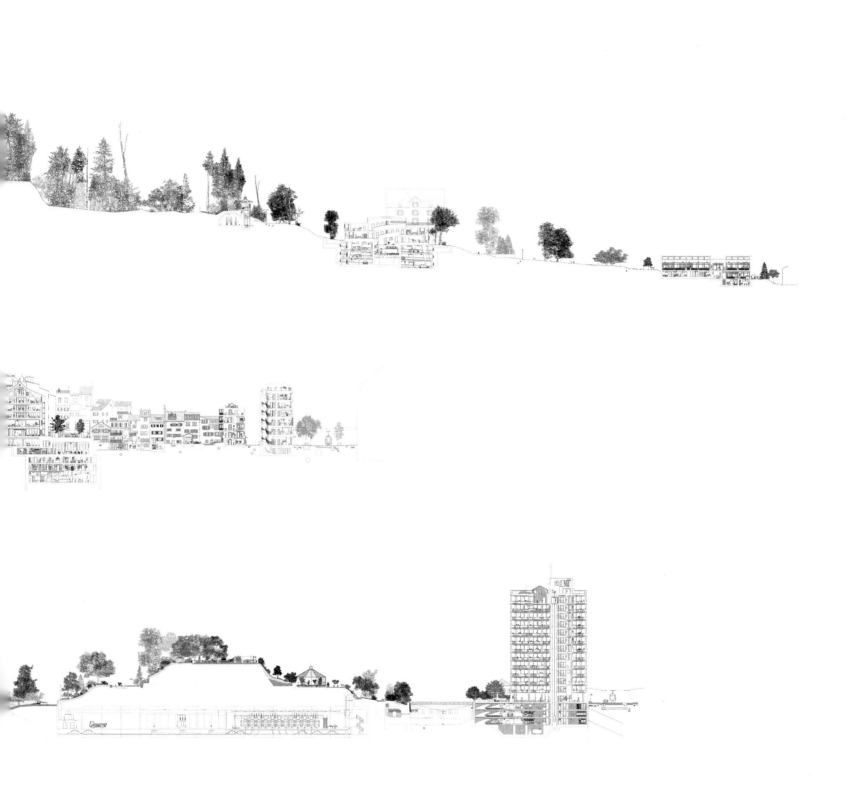

supply shop, a bank and a gym have in common? Or an optometrist, an accountant's office and an empty apartment? At first perhaps, very little. But when you cut through Zurich in section, the survey reveals the intersections and juxtapositions of these places – above, below and within one another. Moreover, when we 'cut' through the city we see its networks and conduits (energy, data, transport) – in other words the infrastructure required for modern life to function.

*pl. 53*  Chair of the Theory of Architecture, ETH Zurich, sections through Altstadt, Zurich, 2021. CAD Drawing

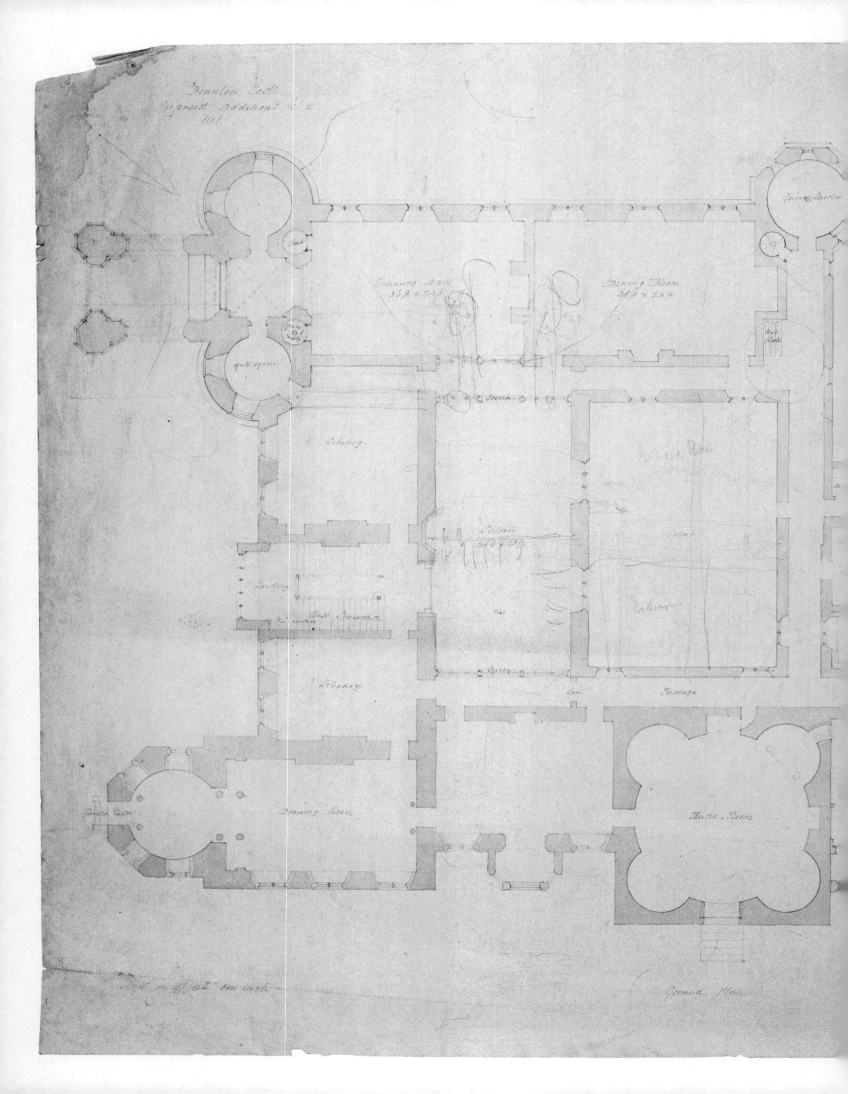

pl. 54 Office of John Nash, proposed additions to Downton Castle, 1808. Pencil, grey and pink wash on wove paper, 380 × 550 mm

Every January, when John Tuomey and I visit Rome, I bring a set of A3 photocopies of the Nolli plan. Every day I mark the routes of my walks through the city using a different coloured pencil. For me this map has a physical presence. It describes the city as I experience it; it also affects how I experience it, sending me into places I wouldn't otherwise notice. One thing leads to another; I find myself in an interesting place and check it on the Nolli plan. It's nearly always there or, if not, some trace of what Nolli drew is discernible in the present fabric. And inevitably beside it on the map is something else of interest; every shift in the angle of a line, every bend and setback, represents a reality that he measured and that I can still experience today.

Nolli's was the first really detailed, carefully surveyed, accurately scaled plan map of Rome. Many good earlier maps were three-dimensional, perspective views. These tended to emphasise the monuments and important landmarks and not to show the background fabric. They were also directional, seen from a viewpoint selected by the mapmaker, with the depicted buildings blocking out whatever was just behind them. Paradoxically, even though it is shown in plan, Nolli's map is a more spatial and three-dimensional representation of the urban fabric. He places the monuments in the context of the dense fabric of the city, correctly records their scale and shows the spaces they do or don't carve out around them. The few obvious mistakes – everyone points to his misalignment of the Theatre of Pompey – just make the accuracy of the whole all the more impressive. This document endures as an accurate representation of Rome, and Rome endures as the city Nolli measured in the 1700s. I am walking in his footsteps.  *Sheila O'Donnell*

pl. 55–56   Sheila O'Donnell, drawing over Giambattista Nolli's *Nuova Topografia di Roma*, 2020. Coloured pencil on photocopy, 297 × 420 mm. Courtesy the architect

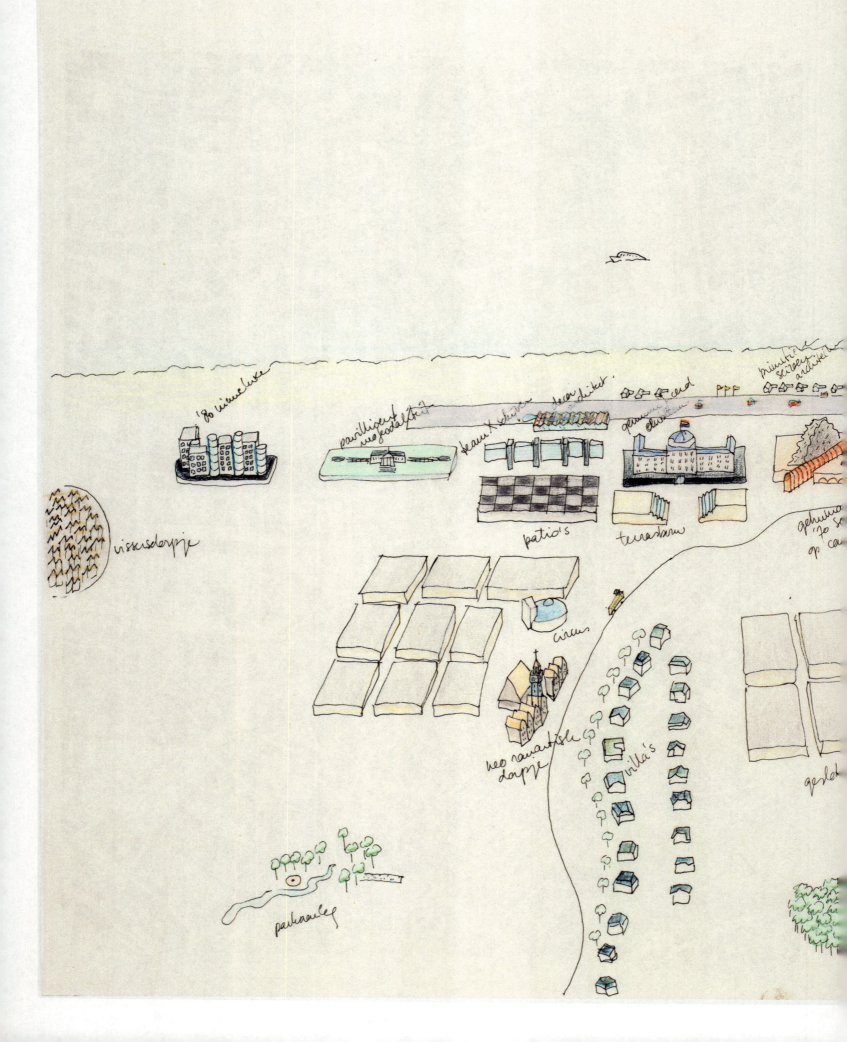

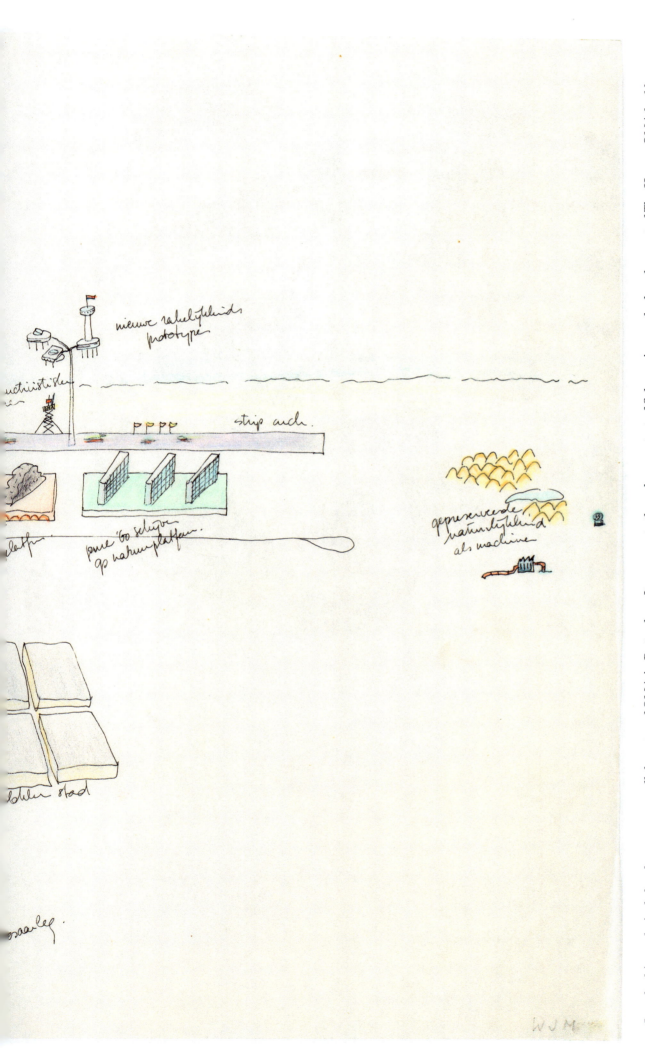

I made this analytical sketch as a young collaborator of OMA in Rotterdam. It represents the urban context of Scheveningen, the beach resort of The Hague. OMA had been commissioned to convert the existing 'Circustheater' in Scheveningen as the new base for the Netherlands Dance Theatre, but in 1983 the city decided to move the NDT to the centre of The Hague and merge it with a proposed hall at the Spuiplein. This combined project opened in 1987, OMA's first major public building. The purpose of this drawing was to analyse the peculiar twentieth-century urban context of Scheveningen. While the beach resort once had lively public spaces, by the 1970s it had fallen victim to poor management by commercial developers. This drawing shows the North Sea at the top and the 'Circustheater' in the centre. There are no design proposals here. The sketch is instead a characterisation of the typologies of the existing building blocks. We had developed a straightforward style of cartoon-like drawing that served our analytical method and was in conscious opposition to the serious and often pretentious architectural drawings of that period, which were mystifying architecture rather than communicating it.   *Willem Jan Neutelings*

*pl.* 57   Willem Jan Neutelings (OMA), typological study of Scheveningen, The Hague, 1982. Ink and crayon on tracing paper, 297 × 420 mm

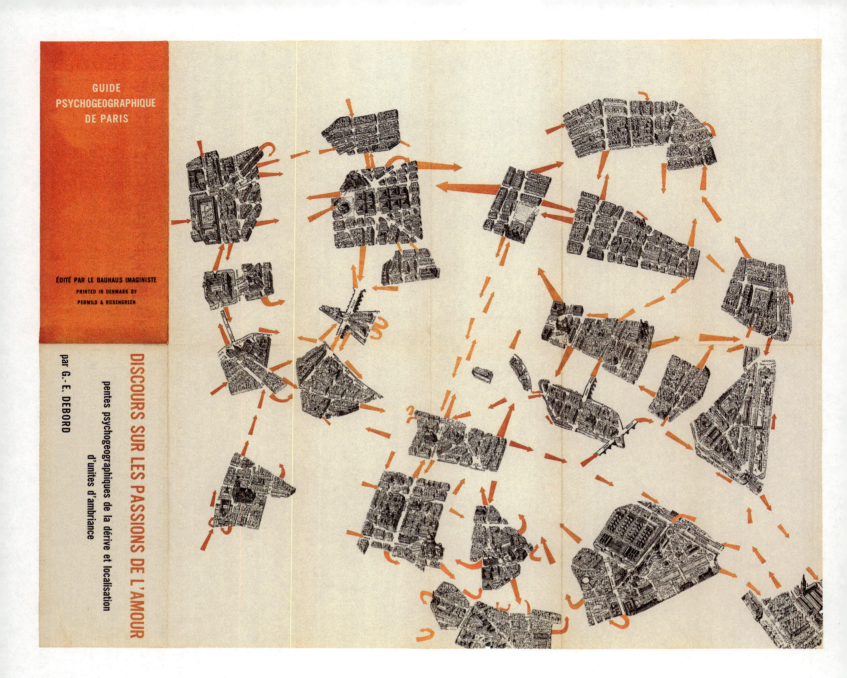

*pl. 58*  Guy Debord, *Guide Psychogeographique de Paris. Discours sur les Passions de l'Amour*, 1957. Lithograph, 595×735 mm

What constitutes a survey – an accurate measurement, a corporeal engagement with place (walking the site), or a gathering together of potential threads from a particular location and also from memory? My rough Clandeboye survey embodies many of these readings. From memory it ushered up and buried in the forest (right) Ledoux's Charcoal Burners' house at Chaux, laying bare my ambition to insert a family of scripted follies in the grounds of Lord and Lady Dufferin's estate between Belfast and Bangor, County Down, Ulster.

    I had tramped the grounds with my AA Diploma students, who were projecting Clandeboye's futures. This sketch is a topographical ordering and a first identification of potential points for intervention. The Georgian house is at the centre, with its front lawn intuited as a rectangle (croquet lawn left – where I shamed myself by breaking a mallet). Behind the house are two more rectangles – stable yards and walled garden. Peripheral forests are darker or scribbled out. Rotating the page 90 degrees to the left edge shows the horizon, broken by Helen's Tower. Meandering through the left forest is Maureen's River where two existing bridges were in bad shape. The sketch agitates here in expectation of my two subsequent bridge proposals – the Divided Bridge and the One Lady Bridge. It also places a viewer at ground level (bottom right corner). Just above him and facing the reedy lake is a rustic boathouse with adjacent Artist's Pavilion. The detailed drawing of this has in the intervening years become a yardstick for the tectonic and figurative themes we were then researching.  *Peter Wilson*

*pl. 59*   Peter Wilson, group of drawings for projects at Clandeboye, 1984. Pen, ink, wash and green crayon on brown card, 300 × 300 mm

The Architecture Iconographies series considers the image-making of architecture through its typologies and unique approaches to drawing. Exploring their resonance in the history of the profession, as well as their relationship to the architects themselves, the series aims to open up further possibilities for their use in both practice and teaching.

*Matthew Wells* teaches the history and theory of architecture at the gta Institute, ETH Zurich. He studied architecture and art history in Liverpool and London. His writing focuses on representational techniques, environmental technologies, and professionalism in the built environment of the nineteenth and twentieth centuries. He was awarded the Theodor-Fischer-Preis in 2019 and commended in the RIBA President's Awards for Research in 2017. *Survey* is his first book.

*Architecture Iconographies – Survey* by Matthew Wells
is published by Drawing Matter and Park Books

With thanks to Niall Hobhouse, Sarah Handelman, Pamela Johnston, Matthew Page, Craig Stevens, Susie Dowding, Lewis Ronald and Mathias Clottu; Neil Bingham, Tobias Erb, Adrian Forty, Emma Letizia Jones, Frank Salmon, Laurent Stalder, Victoria West, India Whiteley, Alessia Zambon. Thanks also to the architects who contributed texts and drawings to the plates section, especially Biba Dow, Tom Emerson, Stephanie Macdonald, Willem Jan Neutelings, Sheila O'Donnell, Thomas Padmanabhan, Eric Parry, Denise Scott Brown, David Valinsky, Lucas Wilson, and Peter Wilson.

*Edited by* Sarah Handelman
*Design and production by* Studio Mathias Clottu
*Cover and section photography by* Lewis Ronald
*Copyediting by* Pamela Johnston
*Printed by* DZA Druckerei zu Altenburg GmbH, Thuringia

© 2021 Matthew Wells, Drawing Matter and Park Books AG, Zurich
© for the texts: the authors
© for the images: Drawing Matter (photography Craig Stevens), except where noted in captions (eg, 'courtesy the architect'). Every effort has been made to trace the copyright holders and obtain permission to reproduce this material.

Drawing Matter
Shatwell Lane
Yarlington
Wincanton BA9 8DL
United Kingdom
drawingmatter.org

Park Books
Niederdorfstrasse 54
8001 Zurich
Switzerland
park-books.com

Park Books is supported by the Federal Office of Culture with a general subsidy for the years 2021–2024

All rights reserved; no part of this publication may be reproduced, stored in a retrieval system or transmitted in any form or by any means, electronic, mechanical, photocopying, recording, or otherwise, without the prior written consent of the publisher.

ISBN 978-3-03860-250-7